Mexico

WORLD BIBLIOGRAPHICAL SERIES

General Editors:
Robert L. Collison (Editor-in-chief)
Sheila R. Herstein
Louis J. Reith
Hans H. Wellisch

VOLUMES IN THE SERIES

VOLUME 48

Mexico

Naomi C. Robbins
Compiler
Edited by Sheila R. Herstein

CLIO PRESS
OXFORD, ENGLAND · SANTA BARBARA, CALIFORNIA

British Library Cataloguing in Publication Data
Robbins, Naomi C.
Mexico. — (World bibliographical series; 48)
1. Mexico — Bibliography
I. Title II. Series
016.972 Z1411

ISBN 0-903450-85-2

Clio Press Ltd.,
55 St. Thomas' Street,
Oxford OX1 1JG, England.

ABC-Clio Information Services
Riviera Campus, 2040 Alameda Padre Serra,
Santa Barbara, Ca. 93103, U.S.A.

Designed by Bernard Crossland
Typeset by Berkshire Publishing Services
Printed and bound in Great Britain
by Billing and Sons Ltd., Worcester.

THE WORLD BIBLIOGRAPHICAL SERIES

This series will eventually cover every country in the world, each in a separate volume comprising annotated entries on works dealing with its history, geography, economy and politics; and with its people, their culture, customs, religion and social organization. Attention will also be paid to current living conditions – housing, education, newspapers, clothing, etc. – that are all too often ignored in standard bibliographies; and to those particular aspects relevant to individual countries. Each volume seeks to achieve, by use of careful selectivity and critical assessment of the literature, an expression of the country and an appreciation of its nature and national aspirations, to guide the reader towards an understanding of its importance. The keynote of the series is to provide, in a uniform format, an interpretation of each country that will express its culture, its place in the world, and the qualities and background that make it unique.

SERIES EDITORS

Robert L. Collison (Editor-in-chief) is Professor Emeritus, Library and Information Studies, University of California, Los Angeles, and is currently the President of the Society of Indexers. Following the war, he served as Reference Librarian for the City of Westminster and later became Librarian to the BBC. During his fifty years as a professional librarian in England and the USA, he has written more than twenty works on bibliography, librarianship, indexing and related subjects.

Sheila R. Herstein is Reference Librarian and Library Instruction Coordinator at the City College of the City University of New York. She has extensive bibliographic experience and described her innovations in the field of bibliographic instruction in 'Team teaching and bibliographic instruction', *The Bookmark*, Autumn 1979. In addition, Doctor Herstein co-authored a basic annotated bibliography in history for Funk & Wagnalls *New encyclopedia*, and for several years reviewed books for *Library Journal*.

Louis J. Reith is librarian with the Franciscan Institute, St. Bonaventure University, New York. He received his PhD from Stanford University, California, and later studied at Eberhard-Karls-Universität, Tübingen. In addition to his activities as a librarian, Dr. Reith is a specialist on 16th-century German history and the Reformation and has published many articles and papers in both German and English. He was also editor of the *American Society for Reformation Research Newsletter*.

Hans H. Wellisch is Associate Professor at the College of Library and Information Services, University of Maryland, and a member of the American Society of Indexers and the International Federation for Documentation. He is the author of numerous articles and several books on indexing and abstracting, and has also published *Indexing and abstracting: an international bibliography*. He also contributes frequently to *Journal of the American Society for Information Science, Library Quarterly*, and *The Indexer*.

Contents

Contents

Contents

Introduction

The country of Mexico stretches 2,000 miles from coast to coast, and includes within its borders a wide variety of scenic treasures as well as a wealth of natural resources. The heritage of its people stems from many great civilizations. Before the arrival of the Spanish conquerors, history viewed the rise and fall of many Indian societies – Olmec, Toltec, Maya and Aztec, to name but a few. In today's society can be seen the influence of the early Indian cultures as well as that of the culture of the Spanish and French. The population now comprises 15 percent people of Spanish descent, 60 percent *mestizo* (people of mixed Spanish and Indian blood), and 25% pure Indian (descendants of the early tribes).

Mexico's history from the time of the Spanish conquest has been a turbulent one, including such episodes as the independence gained in 1821 and the Revolution of 1911. Modern Mexico is a blend of twentieth century industrialization and progress on the one hand, and the problems of rapid population growth and continuing poverty on the other. The current economy suffers from instability, caused by the fluctuations in the oil market, which severely affect Mexico's balance of payments and international debts.

The aim of this selective bibliography is to provide the reader with material on all aspects of Mexican life. It is intended for the general reader, the librarian wishing to build a collection, and the serious student of the country. The works selected are all in English, or contain English translations along with the Spanish text. The only exceptions to this may be found in the section entitled 'The Press', which contains a number of important Spanish-language publications. The 640 entries are arranged into 48 subject categories, and in each of these the entries are arranged alphabetically by title. The brief annotations are intended to provide some flavour of the book's contents or intended audience. Those omissions and errors which inevitably occur in a work of this scope are regretted. It is hoped that both general reader and scholar will be led to works which provide the information and knowledge which is sought.

I wish to express my appreciation to the many librarians, both in my home state of New Jersey, as well as in university libraries which I have visited when travelling, who have allowed me to review materials in their collections. My special thanks go to Murray and Steven Robbins who have provided encouragement and support throughout this project.

The Country and Its People

1 **Acapulco.**
J. Grau. New York: Crescent Books, 1978. 95p.
A title in the Crescent Books collection, presenting marvellous colour photographs of Mexico, accompanied by explanatory text.

2 **The dynamics of Mexican nationalism.**
Frederick C. Turner. Chapel Hill, North Carolina: University of North Carolina Press, 1968. 350p. bibliog.
Traces the historical origins of Mexican nationalism, focusing on the Revolution of 1910.

3 **The labyrinth of solitude: life and thought in Mexico.**
Octavio Paz, translated from the Spanish by Lysander Kemp. New York: Grove Press, 1962. 212p.
A collection of nine essays on the culture and character of Mexico by a prominent Mexican poet. This work was originally published in Mexico in 1950, under the title *El laberinto de la soledad*, and revised in 1959.

4 **Mesoamerica: the evolution of a civilization.**
William T. Sanders, Barbara J. Price. New York: Random House, 1968. 264p. maps. bibliog. (Studies in Anthropology).
An anthropological study of the evolution of cultures in Mexico and Guatemala, going back to pre-conquest times.

5 **Mexico.**
Hans Annaheim, Hans Leuenberger. Chicago: Rand McNally, 1969. 116p. maps.
A beautiful volume with numerous photographs, many of them in colour by Henri-Maurice Berney, which describes the geography and people of Mexico.

6 **Mexico.**
Edgar Bustamente. New York: Crown, 1977. 95p.
A lavishly illustrated general overview of Mexico today.

The Country and Its People

7 **Mexico.**
William Weber Johnson. New York: Time Inc., 1961. 161p. maps.
bibliog. (Life World Library).

A general book on Mexico which includes photographs, information on the pro-
nunciation of some place names and commonly used terms, and a little history.

8 **Mexico.**
Robert Marett. New York: Walker; London: Thames and Hudson,
1971. 208p. maps. bibliog. (Nations and Peoples Library).

A survey of modern Mexican life, including a useful biographical 'Who's Who'
section at the end of the book. Illustrated with a number of photographs.

9 **Mexico.**
Edited by Hanns Reich. New York: Hill and Wang, 1967. 124p.
maps.

A handsome collection of photographs of modern Mexico, with a brief introductory survey of Mexican history.

10 **Mexico: a picture book to remember her by.**
Ted Smart. New York: Crescent Books, 1978.

A collection of splendid colour photographs depicting 20th-century Mexico,
intended for the visitor to the country.

11 **Mexico.**
New York: Greystone Press, 1964. 216p. maps. (Illustrated Library
of the World and its Peoples).

A general encyclopaedic volume presenting an overview of the country with
chapters on history, people, music, theatre, literature, etc. Enhanced by many
illustrations.

12 **Mexico City** (México.)
Bob Schalkwijk. London: Spring Books, 1965. 159p.

A photographic essay on the various aspects of Mexico City – pre-Columbian,
colonial and modern. The text and the captions to the photographs are in English,
Spanish and German.

13 **Mexico City.**
M. Wiesenthal. New York: Crescent Books, 1978. 92p.

A collection of magnificent colour photographs showing the sights and life of
modern Mexico City.

14 **The Mexico I love.**
André Camp. New York: Tudor; Paris: Editions Sun Paris, 1968.
133p. map.
All facets of life in Mexico today are represented in this collection of photographs with accompanying text.

15 **Mexico, land of sunshine and shadow.**
Donald Dilworth Brand. Princeton, New Jersey: Van Nostrand, 1966. 159p. maps. bibliog. (Van Nostrand Searchlight Book, no. 31).
A survey of Mexico for the general reader which includes information on, for instance, geography, economics, foreign relations, and people (race, religion, language, education, etc.).

16 **Mexico today.**
John Armstrong Crow. New York: Harper and Row, 1972.
369p. maps. bibliog.
An introduction to contemporary Mexico, presenting photographs, statistics, and descriptions of various aspects of society such as the economy, literature and politics.

17 **The other Mexico: critique of the pyramid.**
Octavio Paz, translated from the Spanish by Lysander Kemp.
New York: Grove Press, 1972. 148p. bibliog. (Evergreen Black Cat Book, B-359).
A philosophical and historical essay on the development of modern Mexico and the Mexican national identity, originally published under the title *Posdata*.

18 **Profile of man and culture in Mexico.**
Samuel Ramos, translated from the Spanish by Peter G. Earle.
Austin, Texas: University of Texas Press, 1969. 3rd ed. 198p.
(Texas Pan-American Series).
A study of the Mexican national identity, founded as it is in the cultural and educational history of the country.

19 **The roots of *lo-mexicana*: self and society in Mexican thought. 1900-1934.**
Henry C. Schmidt. College Station, Texas: Texas A & M University Press, 1978. 195p. bibliog.
A study of the Mexican search for identity and self-awareness, which formed a base for the nationalism that followed.

20 **Six faces of Mexico: history, people, geography, government, economy, literature and art.**
Edited by Russell C. Ewing. Tucson, Arizona: University of Arizona Press, 1966. 320p. maps. bibliog.

A good general survey, with illustrated essays by six authors on the various facets of modern Mexico.

21 **Sons of the shaking earth.**
Eric Robert Wolf. Chicago: University of Chicago Press, 1959. 303p. maps. bibliog.

Written by an anthropologist, this work will appeal to both the layman and the scholar. Included is much valuable information on the geography, history, religion, political history and sociology of the region known as Mesoamerica (of which Mexico is a large part).

22 **The X in Mexico: growth within tradition.**
Irene Nicholson. Garden City, New York: Doubleday, 1966. 295p. maps. bibliog.

An introduction to, and interpretation of, Mexican tradition and history, written for the general reader and potential visitor.

Geography

General

23 **The central desert of Baja California: demography and ecology.**
Homer Aschmann. Riverside, California: Manessier, 1967. 315p.
maps. bibliog.
Reprint of a 1959 study, containing much useful information on the area.

24 **A guide to the historical geography of New Spain.**
Peter Gerhard. New York: Cambridge University Press, 1972.
476p. maps. bibliog. (Cambridge Latin American Studies, no. 14).
A geographical guide to the changing map of Mexico between 1521 and 1821.
The area covered today makes up central and southern Mexico, excluding the
Yucatán.

Maps and Atlases

25 **Atlas of Mexico.**
Edited by Stanley A. Arbingast and others. Austin, Texas:
University of Texas, Bureau of Business Research, 1975. 2nd ed.
164p. maps.
A useful collection of maps, giving data on physical setting, population, agriculture, industry, transportation and trade. This edition updates and expands the
first, which appeared in 1970.

26 **Political essay on the kingdom of New Spain.**
Alexander von Humboldt, translated from the French by
John Black. New York: AMS Press, 1966. 3 vols. maps.
Reprint of a classic work in the field of the geography of Mexico. Included are
detailed maps based on astronomical and mathematical measurements.

5

Exploration and travel

27 **An American in Maximilian's Mexico, 1865-1866: the diaries of William Marshall Anderson.**
William Marshall Anderson, edited by Ramón Eduardo Ruiz.
San Marino, California: Huntington Library, 1959. 132p. map.
bibliog. (Huntington Library Publications).
The diaries of an American archaeologist in Mexico commissioned by Maximilian in 1865 to survey Coahuila for colonization by the Confederates. An excellent picture of the times during the Juárez-Maximilian era in Mexico.

28 **Anahuac: or Mexico and Mexicans, ancient and modern.**
Edward Burnett Tylor. New York: Bergman Publishers, 1970.
344p. map.
Description of a journey in Mexico made by the author and companions, largely on horseback, between March and June 1856. A reprint of the 1861 edition.

29 **Clemente Guillén, explorer of the South: diaries of the overland expeditions to Bahía Magdalena and La Paz, 1719, 1720-1721.**
Clemente Guillén, translated from the Spanish and edited by
W. Michael Mathes. Los Angeles: Dawson's Book Shop, 1979.
99p. map. (Baja California Travels Series, no. 42).
The diaries of a priest-explorer, Father Clemente Guillén de Castro, who was sent in 1719 to establish a land route from the gulf to Bahía Magdalena and San Bernabé.

30 **The Cora Indians of Baja California: the *relación* of Ignacio María Nápoli, September 20, 1721.**
Ignacio María Nápoli, translated from the Spanish and edited by
James Robert Moriarty III and Benjamin F. Smith. Los Angeles:
Dawson's Book Shop, 1970. 76p. map. bibliog. (Baja California
Travels Series, no. 19).
The observations of a Jesuit priest in Mexico in the 18th century, with the addition of a short biography of the priest.

31 **In search of the magic mushroom: a journey through Mexico.**
Jeremy Sanford. New York: Clarkson N. Potter, 1973. 176p.
bibliog.
An account of the search by a reporter for special mushrooms found in the mountains of Mexico, and believed to be at the heart of many religious ceremonies. His experiences during this journey are related.

32 **Life in Mexico: the letters of Fanny Calderón de la Barca, with new material from the author's private journal.**
Frances Erskine (Inglis) Calderón de la Barca, edited by Howard T. Fisher and Marion Hall Fisher. Garden City, New York: Doubleday, 1966. 834p. maps. bibliog.
A new edition of a memoir published in the 19th century, and providing a wonderful picture of the Mexico of that time. The work comprises the journals and letters of a Scotswoman who married a Spanish diplomat and travelled in Mexico between 1840 and 1841.

33 **Mexico's magic square.**
Erle Stanley Gardner. New York: Morrow, 1968. 205p. map.
An illustrated description of the northern section of Baja California as explored by Erle Stanley Gardner. He calls this area 'Mexico's magic square'.

34 **Missionary in Sonora: the travel reports of Joseph Och, S. J., 1755-1767.**
Joseph Och, translated from the German by Theodore E. Treutlein. San Francisco: California Historical Society, 1965. 196p.
A travel account by a German Jesuit missionary, rich in descriptions of Mexico City and towns along his route to Sonora, as well as of the Indians of Sonora.

35 **The natural history of Baja California.**
Miguel del Barco. Los Angeles: Dawson's Book Shop, 1980. 298p. (Baja California Travels Series, no. 43).
The observations of an 18th century Jesuit missionary in Mexico, originally published under the title *Historia natural y coronica de la Antigua California*.

36 **Travels in the interior of Mexico in 1825, 1826, 1827 and 1828.**
Robert William Hale Hardy. Glorieta, New Mexico: Rio Grande Press, 1977. 558p. (Rio Grande Classic).
A reprint of an 1829 travel diary by a commercial agent in Baja California. The descriptive account is likely to be of interest to the modern reader.

37 **Unknown Mexico: a record of five years' exploration among the tribes of the western Sierra Madre; in the Tierra Caliente of Tepic and Jalisco; and among the Tarascos of Michoacán.**
Karl Sofus Lumholtz. New York: AMS Press, 1973. 2 vols. maps. bibliog.
A classic report, a reprint of the 1902 edition, which contains the first illustrations of West Mexican shaft tomb figures.

Travel Guides

38 All of Mexico at low cost.
Norman D. Ford. Greenlawn, New York: Harian, 1978.

This and the entries which follow comprise a selected list of the many travel guides which are available. Most contain general information useful to the tourist, such as descriptions of hotels, restaurants and sightseeing attractions, etc. Annotations are included only to point out special features of the individual guidebooks.

39 Fabulous Mexico, where everything costs less.
Norman D. Ford. Greenlawn, New York: Harian, 1973. 14th ed. 192p.

40 Fodor's budget Mexico '81.
Eugene Fodor. New York: David McKay, 1980. 252p.

41 Fodor's Mexico.
Eugene Fodor. New York: David McKay, 1972- . annual.

42 Frances Toor's new guide to Mexico.
Frances Toor. New York: Crown, 1965. 7th ed. 317p.

43 Living easy in Mexico: living and travelling south of the border.
Hayes C. Schlundt. Santa Barbara, California: Woodbridge Press, 1978. 208p.

44 Mexico: an extraordinary guide.
Loraine Carlson. Chicago: Rand McNally, 1971. 416p. maps. bibliog.

45 Mexico and Central America.
Frank Bellamy. New York, London: Two Continents Publishing Group, Wilton House Gentry, 1977. 224p. maps.

A guide book for the budget-conscious traveller, describing possible itineraries.

46 Mexico and Guatemala on $10 a day.
New York: Simon and Schuster. 1962- .

Frequently updated.

47 **Mexico 1981.**
Edited by Stephen Birnbaum. Boston, Massachusetts: Houghton
Mifflin, 1981. 451p. (Get 'em and Go Travel Guides).
Covers such diversions as fishing and golf, as well as the usual tourist information.

48 **Mexico: places and pleasures.**
Kate Simon. New York: World Publications, 1979. 3rd rev. ed.
408p. maps.

49 **Mexico especially for women.**
Gerie Tully. New York: Abelard-Schuman, 1976. 421p.
A unique guidebook which offers travel information relevant to unaccompanied
women travellers.

50 **The Mexico traveler: a concise history and guide.**
Selden Rodman. New York: Meredith, 1969. 204p. maps.
bibliog.

51 **Mexico vacation travel guide.**
Exxon Travel Club. New York: Travel Vision, Simon and
Schuster. annual.

52 **Sunset travel guide to Mexico.**
Menlo Park, California: Lane Publishing Co., 144p. maps.

53 **Terry's guide to Mexico.**
James Norman. Garden City, New York: Doubleday, 1972.
rev. ed. 833p. maps. bibliog.
A revised edition of the work first published in 1909 under the title *Terry's
Mexico.*

54 **The Wilhelm's guide to all Mexico.**
John Wilhelm, Lawrence Wilhelm and Charles Wilhelm. New
York: McGraw-Hill, 1978. 5th ed. 485p. maps.

Flora and Fauna

55 **A field guide to the birds of Mexico: including all birds occurring from the northern border of Mexico to the southern border of Nicaragua.**
Ernest Preston Edwards. n.p.: The Author, 1972. 300p. maps.

Over 10,000 Mexican birds are described and illustrated in sketches and colour plates. Much useful information on colour, voice and habitat, etc. is given in the descriptions. The birds are arranged by family.

56 **Wildlife of Mexico: the game birds and mammals.**
A. Starker Leopold. Berkeley, California: University of California Press, 1959. 568p.

A beautifully illustrated work on the distribution of animals in Mexico.

Archaeology and Prehistory

57 **America's first civilization.**
Michael D. Coe. New York: American Heritage, 1968. 159p.
maps. bibliog. (Smithsonian Library).
A non-technical account of the archaeological finds relating to the Olmecs in the
hot tropical lowlands of southern Gulf Coast Mexico.

58 **Ancient Mesoamerica: a comparison of change in three regions.**
Richard E. Blanton and others. New York: Cambridge University
Press, 1982. 300p. bibliog. (New Studies in Archaeology).
The societies in three regions, the valleys of Oaxaca and Mexico and the eastern
Maya lowlands, are compared with regard to social history, and particularly to
political and economic development.

59 **Ancient Mexico in colour.**
Ignacio Bernal. New York: McGraw-Hill, 1968. 159p. map.
Sixty beautiful photographs by Irmgard Groth are accompanied by text describing
the period beginning with the Olmecs and ending with the extinction of the Aztec
civilization in 1519.

60 **Ancient Oaxaca: discoveries in Mexican archaeology and history.**
Edited by John Paddock. Stanford, California: Stanford
University Press, 1966. 416p. maps. bibliog.
A scholarly work on the history and culture of ancient Oaxaca, with contributions
by nine authorities in the field. A fine survey of available information, and well
illustrated.

61 **The ancient past of Mexico.**
Alma M. Reed. New York: Crown, 1966. 388p. maps. bibliog.
A general survey of pre-Columbian Mexico, summarizing archaeological discover-
ies and describing art and architecture.

62 **Anthropology and history in Yucatán.**
Edited by Grant D. Jones. Austin, Texas: University of Texas Press, 1977. 344p. maps. bibliog.
The emphasis in this volume is on 19th-century history, but it also includes two papers of importance to archaeologists.

63 **The archaeological ceramics of Becan, Campeche, Mexico.**
Joseph W. Ball. New Orleans, Louisiana: Middle American Research Institute, Tulane University, 1977. 190p. maps. bibliog. (Middle American Research Institute, Tulane University, Publication no. 43).
An important source work on ceramics from the central Maya lowlands.

64 **Archaeological studies of Mesoamerican obsidian.**
Thomas R. Hester. Socorro, New Mexico: Ballena Press, 1978. 210p. bibliog. (Studies in Mesoamerican Art, Archaeology and Ethnohistory, no. 3).
A collection of papers on obsidian artefacts, quarries and technology, etc.

65 **Archaeology of the Morett Site, Colima.**
Clement W. Meighan. Berkeley, California: University of California, 1972. 211p. bibliog. (Publications in Anthropology, no. 7).
A report on pottery and figurines found in the area from the early and late periods, and a discussion of resemblances to pottery from Central and Northern South America.

66 **The archaeology of West Mexico.**
Edited by Betty Bell. Ajijic, Mexico: Sociedad de Estudios Avanzados del Occidente de México, 1974. 252p. maps. bibliog.
A collection of papers presented to the Society for American Archaeology symposium on West Mexico in 1970-71.

67 **The Aztecs: the history of the Indies of New Spain.**
Diego Durán, trans. from the Spanish by Doris Heyden and Fernando Horcasitas. New York: Orion Press, 1964. 381p. maps. bibliog.
A translation of the work of a Dominican friar, Fray Diego Durán, who was a missionary in 16th-century Mexico. His history of the country before the Spanish conquest was originally entitled *Historia de las Indias de Nueva-España e Islas de la Tierra Firme.*

68   The Aztecs, Mayas and their predecessors: archaeology of
     Mesoamerica.
     Muriel Porter Weaver. New York: Seminar Press, 1973. 347p.
     bibliog. (Studies in Archaeology).
A concise account of current knowledge of Mesoamerican prehistory, which
includes information on recent research, and which is enhanced by some very
good photographs.

69   The basin of Mexico: the ecological processes in the evolution of
     a civilization.
     William T. Sanders, Jeffrey R. Parsons, and Robert S. Santley.
     New York: Academic Press, 1979. 2 vols. maps. bibliog. (Studies
     in Archaeology).
A scholarly work on the settlement pattern of a region of pre-Hispanic Mexico; a
volume of maps assists in the clear presentation of data.

70   Casas Grandes: a fallen trading center of the Gran Chichimeca.
     Charles C. Di Peso, edited by Gloria J. Fanner. Flagstaff, Arizona:
     Northlands Press, with the Amerind Foundation, Inc., 1974.
     8 vols. maps. bibliog.
A provocative archaeological interpretation based upon research done at the site
of Casas Grandes in northern Mexico. The period covered ranges from palaeo-
Indian times to 1821.

71   Chronology and irrigation.
     Edited by Frederick Johnson. Austin, Texas: University of
     Texas Press, 1972. 290p. maps. bibliog. (Prehistory of the
     Tehuacán Valley, vol. 4).
A collection of chapters by various authors on 'chronometric dating' and also on
the hydraulics and water control systems found in the Tehuacán Valley.

72   The Codex Nuttall: a picture manuscript from ancient Mexico:
     the Peabody Museum facsimile.
     Edited by Zelia Nuttall. New York: Dover, 1975. 84p.
A good paperback reprint of the Peabody Museum facsimile of a manuscript
found in a Florentine monastery. The manuscript contains historical and genea-
logical information on the Mixtec civilization of Oaxaca. The 1,200-1,400 painted
figures represent the telling in a visual way of the story of 12th-century Oaxaca,
in much the same fashion as history is represented in the Bayeux tapestry.

Archaeology and Prehistory

73 **The conquest of Yucatán.**
Frans Ferdinand Blom. New York: Cooper Square, 1971.
237p. map.
A reprint of a 1926 work which provides a good introduction to the Maya by an
archaeologist-explorer. The work is based on historical sources and is, therefore,
not rendered too out of date by recent archaeological discoveries.

74 **The early MesoAmerican village.**
Edited by Kent V. Flannery. New York: Academic Press, 1976.
377p. bibliog. (Studies in Archaeology).
Chapters are contributed by a number of authors, dealing with two aspects of the
subject: firstly, analytical procedures for studying such an early society, and
secondly, the presentation of a model society based on the data collected.

75 **A guide to ancient Maya ruins.**
C. Bruce Hunter. Norman, Oklahoma: University of Oklahoma
Press, 1974. 332p. maps. bibliog.
A guidebook for the tourist wishing to visit Mayan archaeological ruins.

76 **A guide to ancient Mexican ruins.**
C. Bruce Hunter. Norman, Oklahoma: University of Oklahoma
Press, 1977. 261p. bibliog.
A profusely illustrated volume, which aims to provide such information on the
ancient ruins of Mexico as will explain the development of the civilizations
represented and their works of art and architecture. Not included are the Maya
areas of southern Mexico, which are covered in the previous item by the same
author.

77 **A guide to Mexican archaeology.**
Román Piña Chan, translated from the Spanish by Virginia B. de
Barrios. Mexico City: Editorial Minutiae Mexicana, 1969. 128p.
map.
A popular survey of pre-Hispanic Mexican cultural history, containing many
illustrations.

78 **A history of Mexican archaeology: the vanished civilizations of
Middle America.**
Ignacio Bernal. London, New York: Thames and Hudson, 1980.
208p. bibliog.
An interesting and readable account of the history of our knowledge about
Mexican culture from prehistoric times to the 20th century. The author uses
account of conquerors and travellers as well as sources describing major excava-
tions and discoveries to document his fascinating work.

79 **In the land of the Olmec.**
Michael D. Coe and Richard A. Diehl. Austin, Texas: University
of Texas Press, 1980. 2 vols. maps. bibliog.

An archaeological study of the Olmec civilization of southern Veracruz and
Tabasco about 3,000 years ago. The project was a cooperative effort by Yale
University, the Instituto Nacional de Antropología e Historia and the Instituto
de Antropología de Veracruz.

80 **Indian art and history: the testimony of prehispanic rock**
paintings in Baja California.
Clement Woodward Meighan. Los Angeles: Dawson's Book
Shop, 1969. 79p. bibliog. (Baja California Travels Series, no. 13).

An archaeological study of Indian history in Baja California, based on the evidence
of the life-size rock paintings of humans and animals. The volume is enhanced by
numerous photographs and sketches.

81 **Las Monjas: a major pre-Mexican architectural complex at**
Chichén Itzá.
John S. Bolles. Norman, Oklahoma: University of Oklahoma
Press, 1976. 304p. bibliog. (Civilization of the American Indian
Series, no. 139).

A profusely illustrated volume on the Maya architectural complex of Las Monjas
at Chichén Itzá.

82 **The Maya.**
Vittoria Calvani, translated from the Italian by Bridget Bailey-
Galiotti. Geneva: Minerva, 1976. 144p.

A lavishly illustrated book, seeking to introduce the reader to the culture of the
Mayas as we know it from recent archaeological discoveries.

83 **Maya: the riddle and rediscovery of a lost civilization.**
Charles Gallenkamp. New York: McKay, 1976. rev. ed. 220p.
maps. bibliog.

A survey of ancient Maya civilization which the layman will find readable. The
author explores recent discoveries which have helped us to understand the origin
of this ancient culture, its achievements and its decline.

84 **Maya archaeology and ethnohistory.**
Edited by Norman Hammond and Gordon K. Willey. Austin,
Texas: University of Texas Press, 1979. 292p. (Texas Pan
American Series).

A collection of scholarly papers representing current research concerning the
civilization of the Mayas, both in the field and in the library. These papers were
presented at the Second Cambridge Symposium on Recent Research in Mesoamerican Archaeology, 29-31 August, 1976.

85 **Maya architecture of the Central Yucatán Peninsula, Mexico.**
David F. Potter. New Orleans, Louisiana: Middle American
Research Institute, Tulane University, 1977. bibliog. (Middle
American Research Institute, Tulane University. Publication
no. 44).

Using the site of Becan, Campeche as evidence, the author presents the thesis that
the Rio Bec and Chenes styles fused into a central Yucatán style.

86 **Maya cities: placemaking and urbanization.**
George F. Andrews. Norman, Oklahoma: University of
Oklahoma Press, 1975. 468p. bibliog. (Civilization of the American
Indian Series, vol. 131).

The author, an architect, presents an analysis of Mayan cities from the point of
view of their evolution as expressions of the Mayan view of the world. A beautifully illustrated volume, this work is recommended as a study in archaeology as
well as urbanization.

87 **Maya cities.**
Paul Rivet, translated from the French by Miriam and Lionel
Kochan. New York: Putnam, 1960. 234p.

A well-illustrated study of four groups of Mayan ruins — those at Copan, Palenque,
Uxmal and Chichén Itzá — in which the author presents much information on the
culture of the peoples who lived there — language, beliefs and daily life, etc.

88 **Maya ruins of Mexico in color: Palenque, Uxmal, Kabah, Sayil,
Xlapak, Labna, Chichén Itzá, Coba, Tulum.**
William M. Ferguson and John Q. Royce. Norman, Oklahoma:
University of Oklahoma Press, 1977. 246p. bibliog.

A beautiful pictorial guide to the remains of the Mayan civilization in Mexico.

89 **The Maya world.**
Elizabeth P. Benson. New York: Crowell, 1977. rev. ed. 176p.
maps. bibliog.

A description of the rise and decline of the Maya civilization. A useful appendix
gives travel information for the various archaeological sites which may be visited.

90 **Mayapán, Yucatán, Mexico.**
E. E. D. Pollock and others. Washington, DC: Carnegie Institute
of Washington, 1962. 442p. maps. (Publication no. 619).

An important group of four monographs discussing the post-classic Maya site of
Yucatán. The report is derived from papers published in the Current Report Series
of the Carnegie Institution, and is hence supplementary to these works.

91 Mesoamerican archaeology: new approaches; proceedings of a
Symposium on Mesoamerican Archaeology held by the University
of Cambridge Center of Latin American Studies, August 1972.
Edited by Norman Hammond. Austin, Texas: University of
Texas Press, 1974. 474p. maps. bibliog.

Useful to the student of Mesoamerica, this volume presents a variety of articles on
various aspects of the archaeology of the region, incorporating new approaches in
theory and technique.

92 **Mexican cities of the gods: an archaeological guide.**
Hans Helfritz, translated from the German. New York:
Praeger, 1970. 180p. maps. bibliog.

A helpful source for the visitor to the Mexican ruins described, this guide book is
divided geographically by region to be visited: the Plateau, Gulf Coast and South.
Many beautiful photographs enhance the book, which originally appeared under
the title *Die Götterburgen Mexikos.*

93 **Mexico.**
Michael D. Coe. New York: Praeger, 1977. 2nd ed. 216p. maps.
bibliog.

A study of pre-Columbian Mexico. A chronological table and many illustrations
are included. This edition is an expanded and revised version of the 1962 original.

94 **Middle classic Mesoamerica, 400-700.**
Edited by Esther Pasztory. New York: Columbia University Press,
1978. 197p. maps. bibliog.

A scholarly collection of essays on the Middle Classic period in Mesoamerica,
providing a comparative study of art and cultural history in the area.

95 **Miscellaneous studies in Mexican prehistory.**
Michael W. Spence, Jeffrey R. Parsons and Mary Hrones Parsons.
Ann Arbor, Michigan: University of Michigan, 1971. 170p. bibliog.
(University of Michigan Museum of Anthropology, Anthro-
pological Papers, no. 45).

A collection of papers on the obsidian industry in central Mexico, the textile
industry, and the production of figurines for functional and iconographic pur-
poses.

96 **Monte Albán: settlement patterns at the ancient Zapotec capital.**
Richard E. Blanton and others. New York: Academic Press, 1978.
451p. maps. bibliog.

Monte Albán is analysed as a regional political capital. Five authors contribute
survey data and tabulations to provide conclusions on population and the social
system.

Archaeology and Prehistory

97 **Nonceramic artefacts.**
Richard S. MacNeish, Antoinette Terner and Irmgard W.
Johnson. Austin, Texas: University of Texas Press, 1967. 258p.
maps. bibliog. (Prehistory of the Tehuacán Valley, vol. 2).

A discussion of artefacts fashioned from a variety of materials by early inhabitants
of the area. Materials covered include textiles, stone and netting, etc.

98 **The North Mexican frontier: readings in archaeology, ethnohistory
and ethnography.**
Edited by Basil C. Hedricks, J. Charles Kelley and Caroll L. Riley.
Carbondale, Illinois: Southern Illinois University Press, 1971.
255p. maps. bibliog.

Thirteen earlier articles are reprinted, accompanied by editorial prefaces and notes.

99 **The pottery of Mayapan, including studies of ceramic material
from Uxmal, Kabah and Chichén Itzá.**
Robert Eliot Smith. Cambridge, Massachusetts: Peabody Museum
of Archaeology and Ethnology, Harvard University, 1971.
2 vols. bibliog. (Papers of the Peabody Museum of Archaeology
and Ethnology, Harvard University, vol. 66).

A scholarly work, volume one of which contains the text while volume two
contains tables, charts and sketches.

100 **Pre-Columbian art of Mexico and Central America.**
Hasso Von Winning. New York: Abrams, 1968. 388p.
maps. bibliog.

A collection of illustrations of sculpture and artefacts found in Western Mexico
and Veracruz. The pieces were selected from various private and museum collections, and the illustrations are accompanied by notes on their symbolism and the
cultural setting in which they were made.

101 **Prehistoric Mesoamerica.**
Richard E. W. Adams. Boston, Massachusetts: Little, Brown,
1977. 370p. maps. bibliog.

A well-illustrated, interpretive work on Mesoamerican history, covering the area
which now comprises Mexico, Guatemala, Belize, Honduras and El Salvador.

102 **Prehistoric settlement patterns in the Texcoco region, Mexico.**
Jeffrey R. Parsons. Ann Arbor, Michigan: University of
Michigan, 1971. 390p. maps. bibliog. (Memoirs of the Museum
of Anthropology, no. 3).

A report on an archaeological study of the region; the volume contains site
descriptions and comparisons with other regions in the Basin of Mexico. The
appendices include ceramic analyses and descriptions of the mounds.

18

103 **Prehistoric social, political, and economic development in the area of the Tehuacán Valley: some results of the Palo Blanco project.**
Edited by Robert D. Drennan. Ann Arbor, Michigan: Museum of Anthropology, University of Michigan, 1979. 259p. (Research Reports in Archaeology, Contribution no. 6). (Museum of Anthropology, University of Michigan, Technical Report no. 11).

A series of papers in both English and Spanish presenting reports on various aspects of a field study conducted in the area of the Tehuacán Valley. The object of the study was to further understanding of how complex societies evolve in social, political and economic terms.

104 **Seri prehistory: the archaeology of the central coast of Sonora, Mexico.**
Thomas G. Bowen. Tucson, Arizona: University of Arizona Press, 1976. 120p. bibliog. (Anthropological Papers of the University of Arizona, no. 27).

A revised account of a report originally presented as a doctoral dissertation in 1969.

105 **The shaft tomb figures of west Mexico.**
Hasso Von Winning. Los Angeles: Southwest Museum, 1974. 183p. map. bibliog. (Southwest Museum Papers, no. 24).

A study of terracotta figures from the shaft tombs of West Mexico. The objects are classified according to subject matter, and the reader is provided with a picture of the life and customs of the people who fashioned them.

106 **Silent cities: Mexico and the Maya.**
Norman F. Carver. Tokyo: Shokokusha, 1966. 246p. map.

A profusely illustrated work on twenty architecturally important pre-Columbian cities of the Mexican and Mayan regions. The photographs are accompanied by text in both English and Japanese.

107 **Studies in ancient Mesoamerica II.**
Edited by John Graham. Berkeley, California: Archaeological Research Facility, Department of Anthropology, University of California, 1975. bibliog. (Contributions of the University of California Archaeological Research Facility, no. 27).

A collection of archaeological papers on various aspects of Mayan life, both in Mexico and in other neighbouring Mayan communities.

108 **Studies in the archaeology of coastal Yucatán and Campeche, Mexico.**
Jack D. Eaton and Joseph W. Ball. New Orleans, Louisiana: Tulane University, Middle American Research Institute, 1978. 146p. maps. (Publication no. 46).

This work contains two studies; one is an archaeological survey of the area, the other describes the archaeological pottery of the region. The period covered extends from the late formative to the colonial era.

109 **Teotihuacán.**
Karl E. Meyer. New York: Newsweek, 1973. 172p. bibliog.

A beautiful volume, describing the rise and fall of the city of Teotihuacán and the other civilizations of the area from Olmec to Aztec. In addition to the fine colour and black and white illustrations, the book contains a special section called 'Ancient Mexico in Literature', which includes selections from various authors and scholars.

110 **Tepexpan Man.**
Helmut DeTerra, Javier Romero and T. D. Stewart. New York: Viking Fund, 1949. 160p. bibliog. (Viking Fund Publications in Anthropology, no. 11).

An archaeological study of the Valley of Mexico, concentrating on the geographical conditions in which prehistoric man developed. Much valuable date on Tepexpan Man is included.

111 **Tlatilco and the pre-classic cultures of the New World.**
Muriel Noé Porter. New York: Wenner-Gren Foundation for Anthropological Research, 1953. 104p. bibliog. (Viking Fund Publications in Anthropology, no. 19).

A study of the Tlatilco culture, with a comparison of various sites in Mesoamerica and Central America, as well as comparisons with sites in the Andes and the southeastern United States.

112 **Urbanization at Teotihuacán, Mexico.**
Edited by René Millon. Austin, Texas: University of Texas Press, 1973. maps. bibliog.

This volume presents data gathered by the author and his associates during more than ten years at this great pre-Columbian city. Part 1 contains the maps produced by the project, and part 2 furnishes the background and a view of the initial results of the study.

113 **The well of sacrifice.**
  Donald Ediger. Garden City, New York: Doubleday, 1971.
  288p.
The fascinating story, complete with photographs, of the archaeological expedition which set out to uncover the Mayan treasures in the Sacred Well at Chichén Itzá.

114 **Yucatán and the Maya civilization.**
  M. Wiesenthal. New York: Crescent Books, 1978. 95p.
A collection of beautiful colour photographs by F. Monfort, with descriptive text provided by Wiesenthal.

115 **The Zapotec princes, priests and peasants.**
  Joseph W. Whitecotton. Norman, Oklahoma: University of
  Oklahoma Press, 1977. 338p. maps. bibliog. (Civilization of the
  American Indian Series).
An introduction to the archaeology and history of the Zapotec region, covering the whole period from ancient to modern times.

History

General

116 **A compact history of Mexico.**
Daniel Cosio Villegas, Ignacio Bernal, Alejandra Moreno Toscano, Luis González and Eduardo Blanquel, translated from the Spanish by Marjory Mattingly Urquidi. Los Angeles: Media Productions, 1974. 157p. maps.

An overview of Mexican history written by a group of Mexican scholars (one archaeologist and four historians) for the general public. The individual chapters were originally intended for a television series, and were written for a Mexican audience under the title *Historia mínima de México*.

117 **A concise history of Mexico from Hidalgo to Cardenas, 1805-1940.**
Jan Bazant. New York: Cambridge University Press, 1977. 222p.

A narrative history of Mexico, with individual chapters on each period of modern Mexican history.

118 **The course of Mexican history.**
Michael C. Meyer and William L. Sherman. New York: Oxford University Press, 1979. 696p. maps. bibliog.

A well-illustrated, updated survey of Mexican history, including coverage of social and cultural history as well as the political and economic aspects. A worthwhile addition to public and academic library collections.

119 **The eagle and the serpent: the Spanish and American invasions of Mexico, 1519 and 1846.**
John Millen Selby. New York: Hippocrene Books, 1978. 163p. bibliog.

A description of the events and personalities involved in the two invasions of Mexico, the one by the Spanish in 1519, and the other by the United States in 1846.

120 **Fire and blood: a history of Mexico.**
T. R. Fehrenbach. New York: Macmillan, 1973. 675p. maps.
bibliog.
A readable one-volume history of Mexico.

121 **A history of Mexico.**
Henry Bamford Parkes. Boston, Massachusetts: Houghton
Mifflin, 1966. 3rd ed. 458p. maps. bibliog.
A general history of Mexico, covering the period up to the 1950s.

122 **The Horizon concise history of Mexico.**
Victor Alba. New York: American Heritage, 1973. 217p. map.
A popular history of Mexico, well illustrated and including a chronology.

123 **Many Mexicos.**
Lesley Byrd Simpson. Berkeley, California: University of
California Press, 1966. 4th rev. ed. 389p. map. bibliog.
A history of Mexico which has undergone periodic revisions to take account of
the dramatic changes taking place since it was first published.

124 **Men of Mexico.**
James Aloysius Magner. New York: Books for Libraries Press,
1968. 614p. maps. bibliog. (Essay Index Reprint Series).
A reprint of a 1942 work which provides a series of biographical sketches of
notable men in Mexican history.

125 **The Mexican nation: a history.**
Herbert Ingram Priestley. New York: Cooper Square Publishers,
1969. 507p. map. (Library of Latin-American History and
Culture).
A reprint of a work originally published in 1923.

126 **The Mexicans: the making of a nation.**
Victor Alba. New York: Praeger, 1967. 268p. maps. bibliog.
A political and social history of Mexico written by a man who went to Mexico
from Spain and lived there for twenty years before embarking on this account.

127 **Mexico.**
Peter Calvert. New York: Praeger, 1973. 361p. maps. bibliog.
(Nations of the Modern World Series).
A work on the history of Mexico aimed at the general reader. Photographs,
biographies and quotations are included, woven into the basic narrative.

128 **Mexico.**
  Robert E. Quirk. Englewood Cliffs, New Jersey: Prentice-Hall,
  1971. 152p. bibliog. (Modern Nations in Historical Perspective).
The volumes in the series to which this book belongs attempt to study past
influences on the present-day politics, social conditions and economic behaviour
of the nation concerned.

129 **Mexico, land of eagle and serpent.**
  Betty Ross. New York: Roy Publishers, 1965. 104p. bibliog.
A short summary of Mexican history from ancient times to the present.

130 **Mexico: a short history.**
  Nicholas Cheetham. New York: Crowell, 1971. 302p. maps.
A well-written survey of Mexican history from 2,000 B.C. to 1969, written by
a former British ambassador to Mexico (1954-1968), which would form a useful
addition to both academic and public libraries. Published in the UK under the
title *A History of Mexico.*

131 **Mexico: the struggle for modernity.**
  Charles Curtis Cumberland. New York: Oxford University Press,
  1968. 394p. maps. bibliog. (Latin American Histories).
A very good introductory text on the economic, social and political history of
Mexico.

132 **Mexico City.**
  Robert Payne. New York: Harcourt, Brace and World, 1968.
  212p.
A beautifully illustrated volume tracing the history of the Mexico City area from
Aztec times to the present.

133 **Middle America: a culture history of heartland and frontiers.**
  Mary W. Helms. Englewood Cliffs, New Jersey: Prentice-Hall,
  1975. 367p. map. bibliog.
An excellent survey of cultural history, comparing developments in central
Mexico and Guatemala with those in lower Central America and northern Mexico.
The student beginning his investigations in this field, as well as the scholar, will
find useful information in this source.

134 **The political evolution of the Mexican people.**
  Justo Sierra, translated from the Spanish by Charles Ramsdell.
  Austin, Texas: University of Texas Press, 1969. 406p. (Texas
  Pan-American Series).
An account of Mexican history written when Porfirio Díaz was in power. The
translation is based on Edmundo O'Gorman's 1848 Spanish edition, entitled
Evolución politica del pueblo mexicano.

135   **San José de Gracia: Mexican village in transition.**
Luis González, translated from the Spanish by John Upton.
Austin, Texas: University of Texas Press, 1974. 362p. maps.
bibliog.
An excellent local history which won an AHA prize for the outstanding historical
work written by a Latin American. The town's evolution is traced from the 1790s
to the present, using written records, oral accounts, and the author's own
memories.

136   **A short history of Mexico.**
John Patrick McHenry. Garden City, New York: Doubleday,
1962. 240p. bibliog. (Dolphin Books, no. C363).
A readable concise history of Mexico in paperback which includes a glossary and
a list of Mexican rulers.

The Conquest (1519-1540)

137   **The Bernal Díaz chronicle: the true story of the conquest of
Mexico.**
Bernal Díaz del Castillo, translated from the Spanish by Albert
Idell. Garden City, New York: Doubleday, 1956. 414p. maps.
The chronicles of one of the *conquistadores* who fought with Cortés, originally
entitled *Historia verdadera de la conquista de la Nueva España*. This translation
is based on a modern Spanish version first published in Mexico in 1950. The
conquest of Mexico by the Spaniards is presented clearly through the eyes of a
contemporary who was involved in the events described.

138   **The broken spears: the Aztec account of the conquest of Mexico.**
Edited by Miguel Léon Portilla, translated from the Spanish by
Lysander Kemp. Boston, Massachusetts: Beacon Press, 1962.
168p. maps. bibliog.
A collection of excerpts from manuscripts and other source materials providing
accounts by native Aztec writers of the conquest of Mexico by Cortés between
1519 and 1521, originally translated from Nahuatl into Spanish by Angel Maria
Garibay K.

139   **The conquest and colonization of Yucatán, 1517-1550.**
Robert Stone Chamberlain. New York: Octagon Books, 1966.
365p. maps. bibliog.
A well-documented history of the Spanish conquest and colonization of Yucatán.
This is a reprint of the 1948 edition, which was first issued as Carnegie Institution
of Washington Publication no. 582.

140   **The conquistadors.**
Hammond Innes. New York: Knopf, 1969. 336p. maps.

A well-illustrated account of the Spanish conquest of Mexico which will enhance any collection, especially on account of its photographs.

141   **The conquistadors: first-person accounts of the conquest of Mexico.**
Edited and translated by Patricia de Fuentes. New York: Orion Press, 1963. 250p. maps. bibliog.

An extremely readable account of the conquest of Mexico as revealed by seven eye-witness accounts. This edition includes documents and illustrations which give the Indian as well as the Spanish viewpoint.

142   **Conquistadors in North American history.**
Paul Horgan. New York: Farrar Straus and Giroux, 1963. 303p. maps. bibliog.

Much interesting information about Mexico is included in this account of the exploration and exploitation of the New World by the Spaniards.

143   **Cortés.**
William Weber Johnson. Boston, Massachusetts: Little, Brown, 1975. 238p. bibliog. (Library of World Biography).

A popular biography of Cortés describing his conquest of the Aztec Empire in Mexico.

144   **Cortés: the life of the conqueror by his secretary.**
Francisco López de Gómara, edited and translated from the Spanish by Lesley Byrd Simpson. Berkeley, California: University of California Press, 1964. 425p. bibliog.

A translation of a work written in 1552 dealing with the life of Cortés, and showing also the life of the Aztecs whom he conquered.

145   **Cortés and Montezuma.**
Maurice Collis. New York: Harcourt, Brace, 1955. 256p.

A readable narrative, designed for the general reader. The author presents an account of the conquest of Mexico from 1518 to 1521.

146   **Cortés and the Aztec conquest.**
Irwin R. Blacker and the Editors of Horizon Magazine. New York: American Heritage, 1965. 153p. map. bibliog. (Horizon Caravel Book).

A popularized, beautifully illustrated work, with a narrative text.

147 **Cortés and the downfall of the Aztec Empire: a study in a conflict of cultures.**
Jon Manchip White. New York: St. Martin's Press, 1971. 352p. maps. bibliog.

Aimed at the general reader by an author well versed in literary style, this is an account of Cortés and the conquest of the Aztec empire.

148 **The discovery and conquest of Mexico, 1517-1521.**
Bernal Díaz del Castillo, edited by Genaro García, translated from the Spanish by A. P. Maudslay. New York: Farrar, Straus and Cudahy, 1956. 478p. maps.

Another translation of the work of one of Cortés' conquistadors (see item no. 137). This is a new edition of the 1920 Maudslay version.

149 **Five letters, 1519-1526.**
Hernando Cortés, translated from the Spanish by J. Bayard Morris. New York: Norton, 1972. 388p. (Books that Live).

The five letters included in this volume deal with the conquest of Mexico between the years 1519 and 1526. The introduction provides a profile of Cortés.

150 **The history of the conquest of Mexico.**
William Hickling Prescott. New York: Bantam Books, 1964. 740p.; New York: Dutton, 1957. 2 vols.; Chicago: University of Chicago Press, 1966. 413p. bibliog. Abridged ed., edited by C. Harvey Gardiner. (Classic American Historians).

The above editions are all reprints of a classic which was originally published in three volumes by Harper in 1843.

151 **The history of the conquest of Mexico by the Spaniards.**
Antonio de Solís y Rivadeneira, translated from the Spanish by Thomas Townshend and revised by Nathaniel Hook. New York: AMS Press, 1971. 2 vols. maps.

A reprint of a 1938 translation of the classic 1684 account of the conquest of Mexico by Cortés.

152 **The hummingbird and the hawk: conquest and sovereignty in the valley of Mexico, 1503-1541.**
R. C. Padden. Columbus, Ohio: Ohio University Press, 1967. 319p. maps. bibliog.

A retelling of the building of the Aztec Empire and its overthrow by the Spanish under Cortés. Useful for getting the essence of Spanish colonial rule in Mexico.

153 **Jerónimo de Aguilar, conquistador.**
Marvin Ellis Butterfield. Tuscaloosa, Alabama: University of
Alabama, 1955. 54p. bibliog. (University of Alabama Studies,
no. 10).

A brief study of the life of one of the men who accompanied Cortés during the
conquest of Mexico. Aguilar was a soldier who served as interpreter and intelligence gatherer for Cortés.

154 **Martin López, conquistador citizen of Mexico.**
C. Harvey Gardiner. Lexington, Kentucky: University of
Kentucky Press, 1958. 193p. bibliog.

The biography of a minor figure in Mexico during the period of the Spanish
conquest, Martin López, a follower of Cortés. The author aims by focusing on this
one figure to present the human side of life in 16th-century Mexico.

The Spanish colonial period (1540-1810)

155 **Naval power in the conquest of Mexico.**
Clinton Harvey Gardiner. Austin, Texas: University of
Texas Press, 1956. 253p. maps. bibliog.

A study of the naval dimension in the conquest of Mexico, with reference to ship-
building as well as the battles.

The Spanish colonial period (1540-1810)

156 **Antonio de Mendoza, first viceroy of New Spain.**
Arthur Scott Aiton. New York: Russell and Russell, 1967.
240p. maps. bibliog.

A reprint of the 1927 edition of a biography of Antonio de Mendoza which concentrates on the development of New Spain during his term of office between
1535 and 1550.

157 **The army in Bourbon Mexico, 1760-1810.**
Christon I. Archer. Albuquerque, New Mexico: University
of New Mexico Press, 1978. 366p. bibliog.

An excellent study of the Spanish army in Mexico between 1760 and 1810, which
provides a picture of Mexico in the Bourbon period as well as a military history.

158 **Baroque times in old Mexico: seventeenth-century persons, places and practices.**
Irving Albert Leonard. Ann Arbor, Michigan: University of Michigan Press, 1959. 260p. maps. bibliog.

A scholarly work which examines the cultural life of 17th century Mexico. Included are entire chapters devoted to intellectual leaders of their time.

159 **Beyond the codices: the Nahua view of colonial Mexico.**
Edited by Arthur J. O. Anderson, Frances Berdan and James Lockhart. Berkeley, California: University of California Press, 1976. 235p. bibliog. (California University at Los Angeles, UCLA Latin American Studies Series, vol. 27).

A presentation of original documents in the Nahuatl language which are important in the study of the colonial period in Mexico, especially the 16th and 17th centuries. English translations are given with the original documents, as well as some early Spanish translations, and the differences in viewpoint between the Indians and the Spanish in Mexico during this period are made very clear.

160 **The century after Cortés.**
Fernando Benitez, translated from the Spanish by Joan Maclean. Chicago: University of Chicago Press, 1965. 296p. bibliog.

A discussion of a period in Mexican history less well known than the time of the conquest by Cortés – the later 16th century, which saw the formation of the first generation Spanish families born in Mexico, the Creoles. Originally entitled *Los primeros Mexicanos: la vida Criolla en el siglo XVI.*

161 **The *encomienda* in New Spain; the beginning of Spanish Mexico.**
Lesley Byrd Simpson. Berkeley, California: University of California Press, 1966. rev. ed. 263p. map. bibliog.

A study of the life and significance of the *encomienda* in colonial Mexico, with reference to many documents.

162 **The forging of the cosmic race: a reinterpretation of colonial Mexico.**
Colin M. MacLachlan and Jaime E. Rodríguez O. Berkeley, California: University of California Press, 1980. 362p. maps.

A controversial interpretation of Mexican history, attempting to show that the Spanish colonial régime was not feudal or exploitative. An interesting picture of the economy and social conditions of the period up to 1821.

163 **The *fuero militia* in New Spain, 1764-1800.**
Lyle N. McAlister. Westport, Connecticut: Greenwood Press,
1974. 117p. bibliog.

A study of the role of the colonial army in Mexico from the point of view of its
legal privileges and abuses. This is a reprint of the edition published in 1957 by
the University of Florida Press, Gainesville.

164 **Lancers for the king: a study of the frontier military system of
northern New Spain, with a translation of the royal regulations
of 1722.**
Sidney B. Brinckerhoff and Odie B. Frank. Phoenix, Arizona:
Arizona Historical Foundation, 1965. 128p. maps. bibliog.

A beautiful volume, which provides an examination from the military point of
view of the Spanish presence in northern New Spain, an area including the
American Southwest as well as parts of Mexico. Facsimiles of documents, sketches
and photographs are included.

165 **Life and labor in ancient Mexico: the brief and summary relation
of the Lords of New Spain.**
Alonso de Zurita, translated from the Spanish and with an introduction by Benjamin Keen. New Brunswick, New Jersey:
Rutgers University Press, 1963. 328p. maps. bibliog.

An English translation of the work of a Spanish judge in Mexico during the 16th
century who analysed the economic, political and social conditions brought upon
the Indians of Mexico by the Spanish conquest. He compares life in Aztec Mexico
before the conquest to life under Spanish rule. Included in this translation is a
biographical essay on Zurita's life and details of how his work was received.

166 **The Mexican nobility at independence, 1780-1826.**
Doris M. Ladd. Austin, Texas: University of Texas Press,
1976. 316p. bibliog. (Latin American Monographs, no. 40).

A thorough study of the Mexican nobility on the economic, social and political
levels. Detailed information is provided on properties, investments, social connec-
tions and political stances.

167 **Mexico under Spain, 1521-1556: society and the origins of
nationality.**
Peggy K. Liss. Chicago: University of Chicago Press, 1975.
229p. bibliog.

A study of the Spanish influence on the Mexican population after the conquest.

168 **New Spain: the birth of modern Mexico.**
Nicholas Cheetham. New York: International Publications
Service, 1974. 336p. maps. bibliog.

A readable study of early Mexican history, enhanced by good photographs.

169 **Provinces of Mexico: variants of Spanish-American regional evolution.**
Edited by Ida Altman and James Lockhart. Los Angeles: University of California, 1976. 291p. map. bibliog. (UCLA Latin American Center Publications).
A collection of regional studies of colonial Mexico.

170 **Race, class and politics in colonial Mexico, 1610-1670.**
J. I. Israel. New York: Oxford University Press, 1975. 305p. maps. bibliog.
An account of the period which emphasizes the politics of 17th century Mexico.

171 **Sixteenth century Mexico: the work of Sahagún.**
Edited by Munro S. Edmonson. Albuquerque, New Mexico. University of New Mexico Press, 1974. 292p. bibliog. (School of American Research Book).
Sahagún was a Franciscan monk in 16th-century Mexico, and this book contains eleven papers presented at the Advanced Seminar Program in Anthropology at the School of American Research, dealing with various aspects of his work.

172 **Slaves of the White God: blacks in Mexico, 1570-1650.**
Colin A. Palmer. Cambridge, Massachusetts: Harvard University Press, 1976. 240p. bibliog.
A study of various aspects of slavery in colonial Mexico, such as the status of slaves in society, religious practices, and the Church's attitude towards slavery.

173 **Soldiers, Indians and silver: North America's first frontier war.**
Philip Wayne Powell. Tempe, Arizona: Arizona State University, 1974. 317p. maps. bibliog.
An account of the Chichimeca War, fought between 1550 and 1590 — the longest Indian war in North American history. This was fought between the Chichimeca Indians, primitive and nomadic tribes of northern Mexico and the United States frontier region, and Spanish forces wishing to settle the area.

174 **The southeast frontier of New Spain.**
Peter Gerhard. Princeton, New Jersey: Princeton University Press, 1979. 213p. maps. bibliog.
The second part of a three-volume guide to early Mexico. Volume one (1972) contained a listing of contemporary documents describing the *gobierno* of central and southern New Spain during the period of Spanish rule. This volume covers the *gobiernos* organized during the colonial period on the southeast frontier. A planned third volume will cover the northern province.

From Independence to the early 20th century (1810-1910)

175 **The cactus throne: the tragedy of Maximilian and Carlotta.**
Richard O'Connor. New York: Putnam, 1971. 375p. bibliog.

A readable account of the intrigues and machinations involved in the placing of Maximilian and Carlotta on the throne of Mexico.

176 **Counterrevolution: the role of the Spaniards in the independence of Mexico, 1804-38.**
Romeo Flores Caballero, translated from the Spanish by Jaime E. Rodríguez O. Lincoln, Nebraska: University of Nebraska Press, 1974. 186p. bibliog.

An interpretation of the role of the Spaniards and their expulsion and replacement by the Creoles during the Independence period in Mexican history. The author stresses the economic and political aspects of this subject. Originally entitled *La contrarevolución en la independencia*.

177 **The crown of Mexico: Maximilian and his empress Carlotta.**
Joan Haslip. New York: Rinehart and Winston, 1972. 531p. maps. bibliog.

A biographical study of Maximilian and Carlotta, which is made even more interesting by the inclusion of photographs and the use of contemporary letters.

178 **The eagle: the autobiography of Santa Anna.**
Antonio López de Santa Anna, edited by Ann Fears Cranford. Austin, Texas: Pemberton Press, 1967. 299p. maps.

The first publication in English of the handwritten autobiography of this important figure in Mexican history.

179 **The emergence of Spanish America: Vicente Rocafuerta and Spanish Americanism, 1808-1832.**
Jaime E. Rodríguez O. Berkeley, California: University of California Press, 1975. 311p. maps. bibliog.

An excellent study of an aspect of Latin American history which concentrates on the work of Vicente Rocafuerta (1783-1847) as a representative of Mexico in Washington and London, and as a proponent of Spanish Americanism.

180 **The fall of the royal government in Mexico City.**
Timothy E. Anna. Lincoln, Nebraska: University of Nebraska Press, 1978. 289p. bibliog.

An analysis of the Mexican movement for independence which argues that the outcome was a tremendous compromise between revolution and counterrevolution which satisfied no one.

181   **Guadalupe Victoria: his role in Mexican independence.**
Arthur L. De Volder. Albuquerque, New Mexico: Artcraft
Studios, 1978. 143p. bibliog.
A biography of the first Mexican president.

182   **The Hidalgo revolt: prelude to Mexican independence.**
Hugh M. Hamill, Jr. Gainesville, Florida: University of Florida
Press, 1966. 284p. map. bibliog.
An attempt to analyse the rebellion led by Miguel Hidalgo y Costilla during the
first stage of Mexico's war for indpendence.

183   **Juárez and his Mexico: a biographical history.**
Ralph Roeder. New York: Viking Press, 1947. 761p. bibliog.
A scholarly study of the life of Juárez and the Mexican struggle for independence.

184   **The liberators: filibustering expeditions into Mexico, 1848-1862,
and the last threat of manifest destiny.**
Joseph Allen Stout. Los Angeles: Westernlore Press, 1973. 202p.
map. bibliog. (Great West and Indian Series, 41).
A study of major attempts made by six men after the end of the war between
Mexico and the United States to wrest more territory from northwestern Mexico
and to provide themselves with new dukedoms or republics.

185   **Maximilian and Carlotta: a tale of romance and tragedy.**
Gene Smith. New York: Morrow, 1973. 318p. bibliog.
A well-documented study of the lives of Maximilian and Carlotta while on the
throne. The author provides a lucid description of the era in which they lived.

186   **Mexico and the Spanish Cortés 1810-1822: eight essays.**
Edited by Nettie Lee Benson. Austin, Texas: University of
Texas Press for the Institute of Latin American Studies, 1968.
243p. (Institute of Latin American Studies, University of Texas.
Latin American Monographs, no. 5).
This work is the result of a seminar on Mexican historiography, in which a group
of graduate students investigated the significance of the Spanish Cortés to Mexico
during the period 1809-1822.

187   **The Porfirian interregnum: the presidency of Manuel González
of Mexico, 1880-1884.**
Don M. Coerver. Fort Worth, Texas: Texas Christian University
Press, 1979. 322p. bibliog. (Texas Christian University Monographs in History and Culture, no. 14).
A re-evaluation of the Porfirian period in Mexican history; special attention is
paid to the role of the González administration.

188 **The reform in Oaxaca, 1856-76: a microhistory of the liberal revolution.**
Charles Redman Berry. Lincoln, Nebraska: University of Nebraska Press, 1980. 282p. maps. bibliog.
A discussion of the period of Mexican history known as *La Reforma*, and the challenge that this liberal movement in Oaxaca presented to the evolution of church, army and landlord.

189 **Santa Anna: the story of an enigma who once was Mexico.**
Wilfrid Hardy Callcott. Hamden, Connecticut: Archon Books, 1964. 391p. bibliog.
A reprint of a 1936 biography of Antonio López de Santa Anna which uses source material to portray the times as accurately as possible.

190 **Viva Juárez! A biography.**
Charles Allen Smart. New York: Lippincott, 1963. 444p. maps.
A readable biography of Benito Juárez, giving a picture of the times in which he lived and the unsettled conditions in Mexico which then prevailed.

The War with the United States (1846-1848)

191 **The Mexican War: a compact history 1846-1848.**
Charles L. Dufour. New York: Hawthorn Books, 1968. 304p. maps. bibliog.
A popular history for the general reader.

192 **The Mexican War: changing interpretations.**
Odie B. Frank and Joseph A. Stout, Jr. Chicago: Sage Books, 1973. 244p. bibliog.
The chapters of this book represent articles on the Mexican War of 1846-1848 which appeared in *Journal of the West*, the majority in the June 1972 issue. The editors have added introductory summaries to each article, and have attempted to present a balanced view of the Mexican War, its causes and consequences.

193 **The Mexican War: 1846-1848.**
Jack K. Bauer. New York: Macmillan, 1974. 454p. maps. bibliog.
The author reinterprets the war, using documentary research, with a view to the concerns of Americans in the Vietnam era. He emphasizes the role of domestic politics in Mexico, and especially in the United States.

194 **Mexico views manifest destiny, 1821-1846: an essay on the**
origins of the Mexican war.
Gene M. Brack. Albuquerque, New Mexico: University of
New Mexico Press, 1976. 194p. bibliog.

A description of the attitudes of Mexicans toward the United States prior to
1844, as shown in pamphlets, newspapers and the writings of leading Mexican
figures. The emphasis is on fear and hostility toward the United States, and no
mention is made of any who desired absorption into the United States.

195 **The story of the Mexican War.**
Russell Potter Reeder. New York: Meredith Press, 1967.
184p. maps. bibliog.

A journalistic description of the Mexican War, written in a popular style for the
general reader.

196 **Surfboats are horse marines: U.S. naval operations in the**
Mexican War, 1846-48.
K. Jack Bauer. Annapolis, Maryland: United States Naval
Institute, 1969. 291p. maps. bibliog.

A detailed naval history of the Mexican War, providing much information on
vessels and personalities involved.

197 **To conquer a peace: the war between the United States**
and Mexico.
John Edward Weems. New York: Doubleday, 1974. 500p.
bibliog.

A popular account based upon English-language secondary and published sources.

The 20th century (1910-the present)

198 **The background of the revolution for Mexican independence.**
Lillian Estelle Fisher. New York: Russell and Russell, 1971.
512p. bibliog.

A reprint of the 1934 edition of the work which presents an interpretation of the
conditions underlying the movement for Mexican independence.

199 *Caudillo* **and peasant in the Mexican Revolution.**
Edited by D. A. Brading. New York: Cambridge University
Press, 1980. 313p. map. (Cambridge Latin American Studies).

A collection of essays by historians and sociologists offering a revised interpretation of the Mexican Revolution. This is a scholarly work, useful to college
and graduate students.

200 **Contemporary Mexico: papers of the IV International Congress of Mexican history.**
Edited by James W. Wilkie, Michael C. Meyer, and Edna Mongón de Wilkie. Berkeley, California: University of California Press, 1976. 858p. map. (UCLA Latin American Studies, vol. 29).

A collection of papers presented in Santa Monica, California, in 1973 on various aspects of Mexican 20th-century history. The papers deal with anthropology, economics, education, literature, political science, philosophy and many other topics.

201 **The Cristero Rebellion: the Mexican people between church and state, 1926-1929.**
Jean A. Meyer. Cambridge, England; New York: Cambridge University Press, 1976. 260p. bibliog. (Cambridge Latin American Studies, no. 24).

A translation of the three-volume work published in 1974 in Spanish under the title *La cristiade* which seeks to describe the *Cristeros*, the Catholic guerillas who fought the Mexican Army between 1926 and 1929. This is an excellent sociological as well as historical work. A French edition was also published in 1976 under the title *La christiade.*

202 **The desert revolution: Baja California, 1911.**
Lowell L. Blaisdell. Madison, Wisconsin: University of Wisconsin Press, 1962. 268p. bibliog.

The story of the role of Baja California and Ricardo Flores Magón in the Mexican Revolution of 1910-1911.

203 **The eagle and the serpent.**
Martin Luis Guzmán, translated from the Spanish by Harriet de Onis. Garden City, New York: Dolphin Books, 1965. 386p.

A book which was first published in Spain in 1928 under the title *El aguila y la serpiente*, and has gone through fourteen editions in Spanish, and translations into many languages. It relates the personal experiences of a survivor of the Mexican Revolution of 1910. The author, himself a part of the Mexican and Spanish literary scene, attempts to place his personal recollections in their historical perspective.

204 **Essays on the Mexican Revolution: revisionist views of the leaders.**
Edited by George Wolfskill and Douglas W. Raymond. Austin, Texas: University of Texas Press, 1980. 136p. (Walter Prescott Webb Memorial Lectures, 13).

A collection of five essays by Mexican studies specialists evaluating major leaders of the Mexican Revolution.

205 **Félix Díaz, the Porfirians, and the Mexican Revolution.**
Peter V. N. Henderson. Lincoln, Nebraska: University of
Nebraska Press, 1981. 239p. bibliog.
A political biography of Félix Díaz, nephew of the dictator, Porfirio Díaz, showing
his influence in revolutionary Mexico.

206 **The great rebellion: Mexico, 1905-1924.**
Ramón Eduardo Ruiz. New York: Norton, 1980. 530p. bibliog.
An examination of the economic and social consequences of the régime of
Porfirio Díaz in Mexican history, with a background study of the Revolution's
leaders.

207 **Heroic Mexico: the violent emergence of a modern nation.**
William Weber Johnson. New York: Doubleday, 1968. 463p.
maps. bibliog. (Mainstream of the Modern World Series).
Another well-written account of the Mexican Revolution, including a valuable list
of principal participants and a chronology of events.

208 **The making of modern Mexico.**
Frank Ralph Brandenburg. Englewood Cliffs, New Jersey:
Prentice-Hall, 1964. 379p. maps. bibliog.
A discussion of the Mexican Revolution and its effects, the role of the Church
in Mexico, socialism, agrarian reform, and many other topics relevant to modern
Mexico.

209 **The meaning of the Mexican Revolution.**
Edited by Charles Curtis Cumberland. Boston, Massachusetts:
D. C. Heath, 1967. 110p. (Problems in Latin American Civi-
lization).
A collection of twenty essays representing varying opinions on all aspects of the
Mexican Revolution (religious, agrarian, economic, etc.).

210 **Mexican militarism: the political rise and fall of the revolutionary
army, 1910-1940.**
Edwin Lieuwen. Albuquerque, New Mexico: University of New
Mexico Press, 1968. 194p. bibliog.
This well-illustrated work is based upon archival and other documentary evidence,
and would make a valuable addition to collections on Latin America.

211 **Mexican rebel: Pascual Orozco and the Mexican Revolution, 1910-1915.**
Michael C. Meyer. Lincoln, Nebraska: University of Nebraska Press, 1967. 172p. bibliog.
A scholarly study of the career of the important military leader and of his relations with other figures at the time of the Mexican Revolution (Madero, Zapata, Villa, etc.).

212 **Mexican Revolution: the constitutionalist years.**
Charles Curtis Cumberland. Austin, Texas: University of Texas Press, 1972. 449p. maps. bibliog. (Texas Pan-American Series).
A history of Mexico during the years 1912 to 1920.

213 **The Mexican revolution, 1914-1915: the convention of Aguascalientes.**
Robert Emmett Quirk, Jr. Bloomington, Indiana: Indiana University Press, 1960. 325p.
A scholarly work, written in an absorbing style, which deals with a complex period during the Mexican Revolution, the time of the overthrow of President Huerta, and analyses the forces at work during this period.

214 **The Mexican woman: a study of her participation in the Revolution, 1910-1940.**
Shirlene Ann Soto. Palo Alto, California: R & E Research Associates, 1979. 118p. bibliog.
A study of the participation of women in the Mexican Revolution as documented in newspapers, magazines, pamphlets and books. Most of these sources were found in the Hemeroteca Nacional de México and the Biblioteca Nacional in Mexico City.

215 **Revolution: Mexico, 1910-20.**
Ronald Atkin. New York: John Day, 1970. 354p. maps. bibliog.
An exciting account of the period, written by a British journalist in narrative style, and providing good reading as well as a wealth of information.

216 **The wind that swept Mexico; the history of the Mexican revolution, 1910-1946.**
Anita Brenner. Austin, Texas: University of Texas Press, 1971. 310p. bibliog. (Texas Pan-American Series).
A reprint of a classic work that appeared in 1943 and vividly described the Mexican Revolution. News photographs from the period are included.

217 **Zapata and the Mexican Revolution.**
John Womack. New York: Knopf, 1969. 435p. bibliog.

A scholarly exploration of the role of Emiliano Zapata and the peasants of Morelos
in the land reform struggle in Mexico from 1910 to 1920.

Population

218 **Evolution of the urban population in the arid zones of Mexico: 1900-1970.**
María Teresa Gutiérrez de MacGregor and Carmen V. Valverde.
Geographical Review, vol. 65, no. 2 (April 1975), p. 214-28.
The authors discuss the factors influencing the very great increase in Mexico's urban population in the arid and semi-arid zones.

219 **Mexico's population pressures.**
Marvin Alisky. *Current History*, vol. 72, no. 425 (March 1977), p. 106-34.
A description of the first steps of a national programme of family planning, begun in 1972 by the Mexican government.

220 **The population of Aztec Mexico in 1548: an analysis of the *Suma de visitas de pueblos.***
Woodrow Wilson Borah and S. F. Cook. Berkeley, California: University of California Press, 1960. 215p. bibliog.
(Ibero-American, 43).
A scholarly statistical study on the population of Mexico in the first half of the 16th century. This work was made possible by a document in the Biblioteca Nacional, Madrid, the *Suma de visitas de pueblos por orden alfabetico*, which describes 843 towns in Mexico during this period.

221 **Race and class in colonial Oaxaca.**
John K. Chance. Stanford, California: Stanford University Press, 1978. 250p. maps. bibliog.
Information on the interaction between ethnic groups in colonial Oaxaca and the development of the economy, demographic patterns and, finally, concepts of power and status.

222 **Responsible parenthood: the politics of Mexico's new population policies.**
Frederick C. Turner. Washington, DC: American Enterprise Institute for Public Policy Research, 1974. 43p. bibliog. (Foreign Affairs Study no. 13).

A discussion of the forces which led to the government drive to limit the very high rate of population growth, a drive which began in 1972 under the régime of President Echeverría.

The Indians of Mexico

General

223 **Ancient Mexico: an introduction to the pre-Hispanic cultures.**
Frederick A. Peterson. New York: Putnam, 1959. 313p. bibliog.
A survey of ancient Mexico dealing with all the major peoples who dwelt there: Aztecs, Maya, Totonacs, Olmecs, Tarascans, Toltecs, Mixtecs and Zapotecs. Both the history of the time and the cultural life of the people are discussed in each case.

224 **The ancient sun kingdoms of the Americas: Aztec, Maya, Inca.**
Victor Wolfgang Von Hagen. Cleveland, Ohio: World, 1961.
617p. maps. bibliog.
A presentation of basic information on the three groups – Aztec, Maya and Inca – in areas such as geography, daily life, law, medicine, religion, etc. Information was gleaned both from research, and from quoting other authorities in the field.

225 **The chronicles of Michoacán.**
Edited and translated by Eugene R. Craine and Reginald C. Reindorp. Norman, Oklahoma: University of Oklahoma Press, 1970. 250p. map. bibliog. (Civilization of the American Indian Series, 98).
The translation of the *Relación de Michoacán* or *Description of the Ceremonies, Rites, Population, and Government of the Indians of the Province of Mechuacán,* which was written between 1529 and 1541 by a Jesuit priest and provides information on the Tarascan Indians of the period.

226 **Handbook of Middle American Indians.**
Gordon F. Ekholm and Ignacio Bernal. Austin, Texas: University of Texas Press, 1971. 458p. maps. (Archaeology of Northern Mesoamerica, vol. 10/11, pt. 1/2).
A collection of articles by experts in the field of ethnohistory. Some representative articles include 'The peoples of Central Mexico and their historical traditions', 'Social organization of ancient Mexico', and 'Native pre-Aztec history of Central Mexico'.

42

227 **The image of disease: medical practices of Nahua Indians of the Huasteca.**
Alan R. Sandstrom. Columbia, Missouri: Department of Anthropology, University of Missouri, 1978. 60p. bibliog. (Monographs in Anthropology, no. 3).
A study of the procedures for treatment and prevention of disease developed by the Nahua Indians of Mexico.

228 **Indian education in the Chiapas Highlands.**
Nancy Modiano. New York: Holt, Rinehart and Winston, 1973. 150p. maps. bibliog. (Case Studies in Education and Culture).
A study of child rearing and education in the Tzotzil and Tzeltal communities. Economic skills and a strong worth ethic are stressed.

229 **Indian Mexico: past and present.**
Edited by Betty Bell. Los Angeles: University of California, Latin American Center, 1967. 109p. bibliog. (Latin American Studies, 7).
A collection of papers on Mesoamerican civilization. Included are papers on ecology, agriculture, the Indian during the colonial period, and contemporary integration problems.

230 **The Mayo Indians of Sonora: a people who refuse to die.**
N. Ross Crumine. Tucson, Arizona: University of Arizona Press, 1977. 167p. maps.
The author analyses Mayo revivalism and interprets their maintenance of a cultural identity in terms of an ethnic separateness.

231 **The Mexican Kickapoo Indians.**
Felipe A. Latorre and Dolores L. Latorre. Austin, Texas: University of Texas Press, 1976. 401p. bibliog. (Texas Pan-American Series).
An anthropological study of a tribe of Indians which had its origin in the United States (in Wisconsin). For over one hundred years this tribe has been living in northern Coahuila, 80 miles north of the United States-Mexican border. Conservative in outlook, the tribe had allowed few outsiders to visit or study them for an extended period until the authors painstakingly won permission.

232 **Missionaries, miners, and Indians: Spanish contact with the Yaqui nation of Northwestern New Spain, 1533-1820.**
Evelyn Hu-De Hart. Tucson, Arizona: University of Arizona Press, 1981. 152p. maps. bibliog.
A study of the colonial period and its impact on the Yaqui people in Mexico.

233 **The Mixtec kings and their people.**
Ronald Spores. Norman, Oklahoma: University of Oklahoma
Press, 1967. 269p. maps. bibliog. (Civilization of the American
Indian Series, 85).

A well-documented work on Mixtec society from the approach of the Spanish
conquest to the end of the 16th century. Much detail is given on the rulers of the
time.

234 **The Mixtecans of Juxtlahuaca, Mexico.**
Antone Kimball Romney and Romaine Romney. New York:
Wiley, 1966. maps. bibliog. (Six Culture Series, vol. 4).

A study of the relationship between methods of treating and training young
children and their development as adults, in terms of personality, philosophy,
code of ethics, etc.

235 **Not forever on earth: prehistory of Mexico.**
Shirley Gorenstein. New York: Scribner, 1974. 153p. maps.
bibliog.

A richly illustrated introduction to the culture of pre-Hispanic Mexico. The
cultures discussed are the Olmec, Maya, Toltec and Aztec.

236 **The Olmec world.**
Ignacio Bernal, translated from the Spanish by Doris Heyden
and Fernando Horcasitas. Berkeley, California: University of
California Press, 1969. 273p. bibliog.

A well-illustrated study of the Olmec civilization, including material on the arts,
society and religion, and based upon archaeological records.

237 **A survey of Indian assimilation in eastern Sonora.**
Thomas B. Hinton. Tucson, Arizona: University of Arizona,
1959. maps. bibliog. (Anthropological Papers of the University
of Arizona, no. 4).

A paper discussing three groups of Indians in the Mexican state of Sonora (the
Lower Pimas, the Jovas, and the Opatas), who were said to be the most assimilated
groups native to the area.

238 **The Tarahumar of Mexico: their environment and material
culture.**
Campbell W. Pennington. Salt Lake City, Utah: University of
Utah Press, 1963. 267p. maps. bibliog.

A useful study of the life style of the Tarahumar people of Chihuahua, Mexico,
with chapters on agriculture, food gathering, dwellings, medicinal plants, etc.

239 **Tarahumara: where night is the day of the moon.**
Bernard L. Fontana. Flagstaff, Arizona: Northland Press, 1979.
167p. bibliog.
A beautiful book, depicting the life of the Tarahumar Indians of northern Mexico.
Illustrated with photographs by John P. Schaefer.

240 **The Tepehuan of Chihuahua: their material culture.**
Campbell W. Pennington. Salt Lake City, Utah: University of
Utah Press, 1969. 413p. maps. bibliog.
A study of the way in which the northern Tepehuan people utilize the resources
of their environment.

241 **The Toltecs: until the fall of Tula.**
Nigel Davies. Norman, Oklahoma: University of Oklahoma
Press, 1977. 533p. maps. bibliog.
The author has attempted to reconstruct Toltec history by using existing archaeological records and written sources. He presents the contradictory evidence that
exists, and in many cases offer his own interpretations, which sometimes differ
from those of his colleagues in the field. An interesting study.

242 **Zapotec deviance: the convergence of folk and modern sociology.**
Henry A. Selby. Austin, Texas: University of Texas Press, 1973.
214p.
A study of socio-psychological views of deviance in a Zapotec community as
shown by fieldwork done in 1965-67. Beliefs on such subjects as witchcraft,
sexual practices, homicides, etc. are explained as functions of social position.

The Aztecs

243 **Aztec thought and culture: a study of the ancient Nahuatl mind.**
Miguel León-Portilla. Norman, Oklahoma: University of
Oklahoma Press, 1963. 241p. (Civilization of the American
Indian Series, 67).
An adaptation of a work, originally published in 1956 under the title *La Filosofía
Ndhuatl*, which was based on the translation of more than ninety native docu-
ments. Aztec ideas on man and religion are discussed.

244 **The Aztecs: a history.**
Nigel Davies. New York: Putnam, 1974. 363p. maps. bibliog.
A political history which is aimed at the non-specialist and which will serve as an
introduction to Aztec civilization.

245 **Aztecs of Mexico: origin, rise and fall of the Aztec Nation.**
George Clapp Vaillant, revised by Suzannah B. Vaillant.
New York: Doubleday, 1962. rev. ed. 312p. maps. bibliog.
(American Museum of Natural History Science Series, vol. II).
An illustrated recreation of the Aztec culture as it existed in the Valley of Mexico
from the 12th century to the conquest by Cortés in 1520.

246 **The Aztecs: people of the sun.**
Alfonso Caso. Norman, Oklahoma: University of Oklahoma
Press, 1958. 125p. (Civilization of the American Indian
Series, 50).
A readable, well-illustrated work which will acquaint the general reader with the
Aztec culture and beliefs. Originally published under the title *El pueblo del sol.*

247 **The Aztecs under Spanish rule: a history of the Indians of the
Valley of Mexico, 1519-1810.**
Charles Gibson. Stanford, California: Stanford University Press,
1964. 657p. maps. bibliog.
A scholarly work on the subject, containing a wealth of data in various appendices
as well as illustrations.

248 **The conquest through Aztec eyes.**
Charles E. Dibble. Salt Lake City, Utah: University of Utah
Press, for the Frederick William Reynolds Association, 1978.
28p. bibliog. (Annual Frederick William Reynolds Lecture, 41).
This short work was originally delivered as a lecture and provides a study of Aztec
society as it existed at the time of the Spanish conquest of Mexico.

249 **Flute of the Smoking Mirror: a portrait of Nezahualcoyotl,
poet-king of the Aztecs.**
Frances Gillmor. Tucson, Arizona: University of Arizona Press,
1968. 183p. map. bibliog.
A biography of an Aztec king who died forty-seven years before the Spaniards
arrived in Mexico, and whose accomplishments included skill as a poet, engineer,
codifier of law, and much else.

250 **Life and death in Milpa Alta: a Nahuatl chronicle of Díaz
And Zapata.**
Luz Jiménez. Norman, Oklahoma: University of Oklahoma
Press, 1972. 187p. (Civilization of the American Indian Series,
vol. 117).
An unusual account, dictated in Nahuatl or Aztec, by an Indian woman who lived
in Milpa Alta and grew up during the revolutionary period in Mexico between
1900 and 1920. The book presents the original Nahuatl text facing its English
translation on the opposite page.

251 **Montezuma: Lord of the Aztecs.**
Cottie Arthur Burland. New York: Putnam, 1973. 269p. bibliog.
A beautifully illustrated story of the life of Montezuma, written from the point
of view of the Aztec society of his own time. Good reading for the non-specialist.

252 **The world of Aztecs.**
William H. Prescott. Geneva: Minerva, 1970. 154p.
A well-illustrated history of the Aztecs in ancient Mexico.

The Maya

253 **The ancient Maya.**
Sylvanus Griswold Morley, revised by George W. Brainerd.
Stanford, California: Stanford University Press, 1956. 3rd ed.
507p. maps. bibliog.
A classic work on the history of the Mayan civilization in southern Mexico, as
well as in northern Central America. Included are many helpful illustrations and
diagrams as well as a chart correlating Mayan and Christian chronologies.

254 **The classic Maya collapse.**
Edited by T. Patrick Culbert. Albuquerque, New Mexico:
University of New Mexico Press, 1973. 549p. bibliog. (School
of American Research Book).
A collection of papers presented at a symposium held at Santa Fe in 1970, exami-
ning the reasons for the decline of Mayan culture.

255 **The Codex Pérez and the Book of Chilam Balam of Maní.**
Edited and translated by Eugene R. Craine and Reginald C.
Reindorp. Norman, Oklahoma: University of Oklahoma Press,
1979. 209p. bibliog. (Civilization of the American Indian Series).
A translation into English of an important collection of documents collected by
Don Juan Pió Pérez of Yucatán. These were taken from Mayan sources in order
to preserve material still existing on the Mayan culture and language.

256 **Jinetic Lubton: some modern and prehispanic Maya ceremonial
customs in the highlands of Chiapas, Mexico.**
Thomas A. Lee, Jr. *New World Archaeological Foundation
Papers*, no. 29 (1972), p. 1-28.
A report showing the similarity of modern burial customs and ceremonies to
prehispanic Maya customs practised in the highlands of Chiapas.

257 **Land of the Mayas: yesterday and today.**
Carleton Beals. New York: Abelard-Schuman, 1966.
158p. bibliog.
A simple account of Maya history and culture, with very good photographs.

258 **The Maya.**
Michael D. Coe. New York: Praeger, 1966. 252p. maps. bibliog.
(Ancient Peoples and Places, vol. 52).
Required reading in the literature on Mayan civilization. The author presents an excellent and comprehensive study of the culture as it developed in Mexico as well as in the other areas of southern Mesoamerica.

259 **Maya history and religion.**
John Eric Sidney Thompson. Norman, Oklahoma: University of Oklahoma Press, 1970. 415p. bibliog. (Civilization of the American Indian, vol. 99).
A scholarly work concerned with various aspects of Maya culture and well documented with references to colonial writings and archaeological data.

260 **The mysterious Maya.**
George E. Stuart and Gene S. Stuart. Washington, DC: National Geographic Society, 1977. 199p. bibliog.
A study of the Maya civilization in Mesoamerica, including Mexico, enhanced by the beautiful colour photographs for which National Geographic Society publications are noted.

261 **The origins of Maya civilization.**
Edited by Richard E. W. Adams. Albuquerque, New Mexico: University of New Mexico Press, 1977. 465p. maps. bibliog.
(School of American Research Book, Advanced Seminar Series).
Discussed in this informative volume are the early formative stages in different parts of the Maya lowlands, we well as cultural comparisons between the Maya and their neighbours (Olmec, Mixe-Zoque and Izapa).

262 **The rise and fall of Maya civilization.**
J. Eric S. Thompson. Norman, Oklahoma: University of Oklahoma Press, 1966. 2nd ed. 328p. bibliog.
A study of the Maya as a people, revised and updated to include new material found in more recent excavations. Well illustrated and readable, this is a fine addition to any collection on the subject.

263 **The ruins of time: four and a half centuries of conquest and discovery among the Maya.**
David Grant Adamson. New York: Praeger, 1975. 272p. maps. bibliog.

A history of the Maya Indians of Mexico and Guatemala from the post-conquest period of the 16th century to the present time.

264 **Zinacantan: a Maya community in the highlands of Chiapas.**
Evon Zartman Vogt. Cambridge, Massachusetts: Belknap Press of Harvard University Press, 1968. 733p. map. bibliog.

An ethnographic study of the Zinacanteco way of life in the highlands of Chiapas.

265 **The Zinacantecos of Mexico: a modern Maya way of life.**
Evon Zartman Vogt. New York: Holt, Rinehart and Winston, 1970. 113p. map. bibliog. (Case Studies in Cultural Anthropology).

An interesting study of all aspects of the modern life of the Mayas in Zinacantan.

Language and Dialects

266 **Ancient Maya writing and calligraphy.**
Michael D. Coe. *Visible Language,* vol. 5, no. 4 (1971),
p. 293-307.

An important article explaining the evolution of Maya writing from a pictographic
system to one with phonetic-syllabic elements.

267 **Chatino syntax.**
Kitty Price. Norman, Oklahoma: University of Oklahoma,
Summer Institute of Linguistics, 1965. 248p. bibliog.
(Publications in Linguistics and Related Fields Series, no. 12).

A grammar dealing with the Yaitepec dialect of the Indian language of Chatino,
spoken by an Indian tribe living in southwest Oaxaca, Mexico.

268 **A commentary on the Dresden Codex.**
J. Eric S. Thompson. Philadelphia, Pennsylvania: American
Philosophical Society, 1972. 156p. (Memoir, 93).

This work must be used in conjunction with Thompson's *Maya hieroglyphic
writing* (see item no. 272) and *A catalog of Maya hieroglyphs.*

269 **Deciphering the Maya script.**
David Humiston Kelley. Austin, Texas: University of Texas
Press, 1976. 334p. bibliog.

An important work for students of ancient Maya, as it updates other material on
the deciphering of Maya hieroglyphics.

270 **Generative syntax of Penoles Mixtec.**
John P. Daly. Dallas, Texas: Summer Institute of Linguistics,
1973. 90p. bibliog. (Publications in Linguistics Series, no. 42).

An analysis of Mixtec grammar, originally presented as a doctoral study and
revised slightly for this publication.

271 **The Jacaltec language.**
Christopher Day. Bloomington, Indiana: Indiana University,
1973. 135p. (Language Science Monographs, vol. 12).
A grammar of the Mayan language of Jacaltec, which is spoken in parts of Guatemala and in the Mexican state of Chiapas.

272 **Maya hieroglyphs without tears.**
J. Eric S. Thompson. London: British Museum, Dept. of
Ethnography, 1972. 84p. maps.
An updated version of the author's *Maya hieroglyphic writing.* This work is well
illustrated and emphasizes the use of the calendar and ritual.

273 **Mesoamerican writing systems: a conference at Dumbarton Oaks,
October 30th and 31st, 1971.**
Edited by Elizabeth P. Benson. Washington, DC: Dumbarton
Oaks Research Library and Collections, Trustees for Harvard
University, 1973. 226p. bibliog.
A collection of papers on writing systems used in Mesoamerica.

274 **Nahuatl in the middle years: language control phenomena in
texts of the colonial period.**
Frances Karttunen and James Lockhart. Berkeley, California:
University of California Press, 1976. 146p. bibliog. (Publications
in Linguistics Series, vol. 85).
A study of the language of central Mexican Indian communities during the
colonial period. This book serves the scholar working with Nahuatl documents of
the period, and also examines the influences of Spanish upon the language.

275 **Papago and Pima to English, English to Papago and Pima
dictionary.**
Dean Saxton and Lucille Saxton. Tucson, Arizona: University
of Arizona Press, 1969. 191p. bibliog.
A very useful reference tool for anyone aiming to understand the Papago-Pima
language used by the desert people of southern Arizona and northern Sonora,
Mexico.

276 **Some aspects of the lexical structure of a Mazatec historical text.**
George M. Cowan. Norman, Oklahoma: University of
Oklahoma, Summer Institute of Linguistics, 1965. 146p. bibliog.
(Summer Institute of Linguistics Publications, no. 11).
A study of the structure of the Mazatec language, emphasizing lexical language.

Language and Dialects

277 **Telling tongues: language policy in Mexico, colony to nation.**
Shirley Brice Heath. New York: Teachers College Press, 1972.
300p. bibliog. (Columbia University Teachers College, Center
for Education in Latin America. Institute of International
Studies. Publications).

A discussion of language policy in Mexico, as a social and political issue. The question was whether Indians should be forced to learn Spanish in order to participate in Mexican society; this was an issue during the colonial and early national period.

278 **Yaqui syntax.**
Jacqueline Lindenfeld. Berkeley, California: University of
California Press, 1974. 162p. bibliog. (University of California
Publications in Linguistics, vol. 76).

A study of the syntactic structure of the Yaqui language, spoken by members of the Yaqui Indian tribe living in northwestern Mexico and Arizona.

Religion

279 **Alienation of church wealth in Mexico: social and economic aspects of the liberal revolution, 1856-1875.**
Jan Bazant, edited and translated from the Spanish by Michael P. Costeloe. Cambridge, England: Cambridge University Press, 1971. 332p. bibliog. (Cambridge Latin American Studies, 11).
A study of the nationalization and sale of goods belonging to the Roman Catholic Church in Mexico from 1822 to the end of the 19th century.

280 **Book of the gods and rites and the ancient calendar.**
Diego Durán, edited and translated from the Spanish by Fernando Horcasitas and Doris Heyden. Norman, Oklahoma: University of Oklahoma Press, 1971. 502p. bibliog. (Civilization of the American Indian Series, 102).
A translation of one of the classic studies of the Aztec religion and their calendrical system. Included is a biographical study of Durán taken from his own writings.

281 **Burning water: thought and religion in ancient Mexico.**
Laurette Séjourné. New York: Grove Press, 1960. 192p. bibliog. (Evergreen Book, E-241).
The author, an archaeologist, describes the religion and ethics of pre-Columbian Mexico, based on her finds at Teotihuacán.

282 **The Catholic Church in Mexico: historical essays for the general reader. Vol. 1, 1519-1910.**
Paul V. Murray. Mexico City: Editorial E.P.M., 1965. 398p.
An ecclesiastical history of the Catholic Church in Mexico before 1910, with emphasis on the 19th century.

283 **Church and state in Mexico, 1822-1857.**
Wilfrid Hardy Callcott. New York: Octagon Books, 1965. 357p. bibliog.
A discussion of the struggle between the Catholic Church and the Mexican government which ended with the Constitution of 1857.

Religion

284 **Church property and the Mexican Reform, 1856-1910.**
Robert J. Knowlton. De Kalb, Illinois: Northern Illinois
University Press, 1976. 265p. bibliog. (Origins of Modern
Mexico).
An excellent survey of the nationalization of church property during the Reform
period in Mexico.

285 **Crown and clergy in colonial Mexico, 1759-1821: the crisis of
ecclesiastical privilege.**
N. M. Farriss. London: University of London and the Athlone
Press, 1968. 288p. bibliog. (University of London Historical
Studies, 21).
A scholarly work on the crown's control over the Mexican clergy. Archival sources
are used extensively.

286 **The enlightened: the writings of Luis de Carvajal, el Mozo.**
Luis de Carvajal, edited and translated from the Spanish by
Seymour B. Liebman. Coral Gables, Florida: University of
Miami Press, 1967. 157p. bibliog.
This work contains English translations of the memoirs, letters and other docu-
ments of a young Jew who was executed by the Inquisition in Mexico in 1596.

287 **The gods of Mexico.**
C. A. Burland. New York: Putnam, 1967. 219p. maps. bibliog.
A study of the ancient religion of Mexico, using archaeological evidence, religious
codices and works by post-conquest Spanish missionaries as sources. This book
will appeal to general reader and scholar alike.

288 **The Mexican Inquisition of the sixteenth century.**
Richard E. Greenleaf. Albuquerque, New Mexico: University
of New Mexico Press, 1969. 242p. bibliog.
The author provides new data on the Mexican Inquisition. He illustrates his work
with cases taken from the Inquisition papers of the Archivo General de la Nación.

289 **The Mexican revolution and the Catholic Church, 1910-1929.**
Robert E. Quirk. Bloomington, Indiana: Indiana University
Press, 1973. 276p.
An excellent study of the confrontation between the forces of Mexican nationalism and the Catholic Church at the time of the 1910 Revolution. Material on
the history of the Church in Mexico is included, as well as much material on
people and events during the Revolution.

290 **Mexico mystique: the coming sixth world of consciousness.**
Frank Waters. Chicago: Sage Books, 1975. 326p. bibliog.
A study of the religious and spiritual background of Mexico, as seen in its mythology and symbolism. Also discussed are the concepts of time found in the Mayan calendar and astronomical calculations.

291 **Quetzalcoatl and Guadalupe: the formation of Mexican national consciousness, 1531-1812.**
Jacques Lafaye, translated from the French by Benjamin Keen. Chicago: University of Chicago Press, 1976. 336p.
A scholarly study of the importance of religious beliefs in colonial Mexico, with discussion of the ideas of such groups as the pre-conquest Indians, colonial Creoles, Franciscans and Jesuits.

292 **Religious aspects of the conquest of Mexico.**
Charles Samuel Brader. New York: AMS Press, 1966. 344p. bibliog.
A reprint of a 1930 work dealing with the Aztec religion and the influences of Christianity and the native religions upon each other during the 16th century.

293 **Spanish Jesuit churches in Mexico's Tarahumara.**
Paul M. Roca. Tucson, Arizona: University of Arizona Press, 1979. 369p. bibliog.
A scholarly work that contains much valuable information on Spanish Jesuit churches built in Western Chihuahua between 1611 and 1767. The book is useful both for its architectural detail (including many photographs), and for the religious history of the Tarahumara Indians which it presents.

294 **The spiritual conquest of Mexico: an essay on the apostolate and the evangelizing methods of the mendicant orders in New Spain, 1523-1572.**
Robert Ricard, translated from the French by Lesley Byrd Simpson. Berkeley, California: University of California Press, 1966. 423p. bibliog.
A discussion of the conversion of the Indians and the establishment of the Church in Mexico after the conquest by Cortés, originally published under the title *Conquête spirituelle du Mexique.*

295 **Tortillas for the gods: a symbolic analysis of Zinacantican rituals.**
Evon Zartman Vogt. Cambridge, Massachusetts: Harvard University Press, 1976. 234p. bibliog.
A study of the ritual life of Zinacantan, a municipality in southeastern Mexico.

Social Conditions

296 **Being Indian in Hueyapan: a study of forced identity in contemporary Mexico.**
Judith Friedlander. New York: St. Martin's Press, 1975. 205p. bibliog.

A description of life in Hueyepan (a Nahuatl-speaking community), where, the author shows, being Indian means being poor and oppressed. Little Indian culture survives, and what does survive contains much European influence.

297 **The children of Sánchez: autobiography of a Mexican family.**
Oscar Lewis. New York: Random House, 1961. 499p.

A classic in the field of sociology, this work depicts the life of a poor family in Mexico City in the 1950s. The method used is that of multiple autobiographies, so that life is seen through the eyes of the people themselves.

298 **Conflict, violence and morality in a Mexican village.**
Lola Romanucci-Ross. Palo Alto, California: National Press Books, 1973. 203p. bibliog.

An anthropological study of a Mexican village since the Revolution of 1910, to show the social and moral codes that have evolved. Some examples are the concept of *machismo*, bonds of kinship, patronage, etc.

299 **A death in the Sánchez family.**
Oscar Lewis. New York: Random House, 1969. 119p.

This book should be read as a continuation of the story of the Sánchez family told in *Children of Sánchez*. It relates the life of Aunt Guadalupe and the reactions of family members to her death and funeral. An important addition to collections on anthropology and sociology.

300 **Drinking, homicide and rebellion in colonial Mexican villages.**
William B. Taylor. Stanford, California: Stanford University Press, 1979. 242p. maps. bibliog.

A well-documented social history of central Mexico and Oaxaca, showing the peasant behaviour patterns under stress and under Spanish rule. Court records and archives are used to illustrate the picture portrayed.

301 **Economics and prestige in a Maya community.**
Frank Cancian. Stanford, California: Stanford University Press,
1965. 238p. maps.
A description of a community which has as its basis for the achievement of
prestige a system of conspicuous giving.

302 **Epidemic disease in Mexico City, 1761-1813: an administrative,
social and medical study.**
Donald B. Cooper. Austin, Texas: University of Texas, Institute
of Latin American Studies, 1965. 236p. bibliog. (Latin American
Monographs, 3).
An account of five epidemics in Mexico City between 1761 and 1813. Information
on public measures for control reveals features of late colonial society.

303 **Essays on Mexican kinship.**
Edited by Hugo G. Nutini, Pedro Carrasco and Jane M. Taggart.
Pittsburgh, Pennsylvania: University of Pittsburgh Press, 1976.
256p. bibliog. (Pitt Latin American Series).
A collection of papers on various kinship topics applied to life in Mesoamerica.

304 **Ethnic relations in the Chiapas highlands of Mexico.**
Benjamin N. Colby. Santa Fe, New Mexico: Museum of
New Mexico Press, 1966. 76p. bibliog.
A study of relations between *ladinos* and Indians in San Cristobal and Zinacantan,
Mexico. An appendix shows the questions that were asked in the study.

305 **Five families: Mexican case studies in the culture of poverty.**
Oscar Lewis. New York: Basic Books, 1959. 351p.
A sociological study presenting five days in the lives of five families representing
a cross-section of Mexican life in the late 1950s.

306 **Folk practices in North Mexico: birth customs, folk medicine
and spiritualism in the Laguna Zone.**
Isabel Kelly. Austin, Texas: University of Texas Press, 1965.
166p. bibliog.
A specialized work that should be of interest to medical and anthropological
collections, this is a study of folk practices related to health and healing in
northern Mexico.

307 **Gossip, reputation and knowledge in Zinacantan.**
John Beard Haviland. Chicago: University of Chicago
Press, 1977. 264p. bibliog.
A cultural picture of the Zinacantan area, showing the use of gossip in people's
daily lives.

308 **The incredible city: Real de Catorce, Mexico.**
Lucy H. Wallace. Mission, Texas: Amigo Enterprises, 1965.
116p.

Presents the history of a mining community in San Luis Potosí, tracing it back to 1773, and showing it to be unchanging in the world of Mexico today.

309 **The Isthmus Zapotecs: women's roles in cultural context.**
Beverly Chinas. New York: Holt, Rinehart and Winston, 1973.
122p. map. bibliog. (Case Studies in Cultural Anthropology).

An account of the social position of women in the locality, with reference to marriage, mourning behaviour, the role as mediator in conflicts, and the supplementing of family income by selling in local markets.

310 **Land and society in colonial Mexico; the great *hacienda*.**
François Chevalier, translated from the French by Alvin Eustis.
Berkeley, California: University of California Press, 1963. 334p.
bibliog.

A translation which contributes new interpretations of and scholarly documentation on Mexican colonial history.

311 **Medical choice in a Mexican village.**
James Clay Young. New Brunswick, New Jersey: Rutgers
University Press, 1981. 233p. bibliog.

A study of medical choices available in the village of Pichátaro, Mexico, this work describes the manner in which people in a Third World rural community deal with the treatment of illness.

312 **A Mexican family empire: the *latifundio* of the Sánchez Navarros,
1765-1867.**
Charles H. Harris. Austin, Texas: University of Texas Press,
1975. 410p. maps. bibliog.

A study which enhances our understanding of the large estate (the Mexican *latifundio*), which was composed of two or more *haciendas* and was an important socioeconomic institution before the Revolution of 1910.

313 **Networks and marginality: life in a Mexican shantytown.**
Larissa Adler Lomnitz. New York: Academic Press, 1977. 230p.
bibliog. (Studies in Anthropology).

A sociological study of life in a marginal community, a Mexico City shantytown, and of how this is representative of an element of society in Latin America which must cope with chronic unemployment and survival problems.

314 **Pedro Martínez: a Mexican peasant and his family.**
Oscar Lewis. New York: Random House, 1964. 507p.
An account of the life of a Mexican peasant, born in an Aztec village. The story is told by means of tape-recorded interviews conducted over a period of twenty years. Another in the author's series of fine anthropological works on Mexico.

315 **Politics and the migrant poor in Mexico City.**
Wayne A. Cornelius. Stanford, California: Stanford University Press, 1975. 319p. bibliog.
A view of the life of the poor in Mexico City, using the techniques of questionnaires, charts, photographs and general surveys. An excellent sociological work.

316 **The poverty of revolution: the state and the urban poor in Mexico.**
Susan Eckstein. Princeton, New Jersey: Princeton University Press, 1977. 300p. maps. bibliog.
An analysis of the poor districts of Mexico City, using data from three areas: 1) a city slum; 2) a semi-rural area; 3) a government-financed planned community.

317 **Princes of the earth: subcultural diversity in a Mexican municipality.**
Barbara Luise Margolies. Washington, DC: American Anthropological Association, 1975. 180p. bibliog. (Special Publication of the American Anthropological Association, no. 2).
An anthropological study of a rural community in Mexico and its relationship to the country as a whole during the twenty years following the Mexican Revolution.

318 **Ritual kinship: the structure and historical development of the** *compadrazzo* **system in rural Tlaxcala.**
Hugo G. Nutini and Betty Bell. Princeton, New Jersey: Princeton University Press, 1980. bibliog.
A scholarly ethnographic study of ritual kinship in Santa Maria Belén Cizitzimititlán, Mexico.

319 **Settlers of Bajavista: social and economic adaptation in a Mexican squatter settlement.**
James F. Hopgood. Columbus, Ohio: Ohio University Center for International Studies, 1979. 145p. bibliog. (Papers in International Studies. Latin American Series, no. 7).
A revision of the author's doctoral thesis, containing statistical data to document the work presented.

Social conditions

320 **Social character in a Mexican village.**
Erich Fromm and Michael Maccoby. Englewood Cliffs, New
Jersey: Prentice Hall, 1970. 303p. bibliog.

An excellent work on personality and society in Mexico which describes society's
effect upon social character and ideology. The major character types in a Mexican
village are analysed, and such topics as character formation in childhood and
possibilities for change are dealt with.

321 **Synoptic studies of Mexican culture.**
Munro Edmonson, Glen Fisher, Pedro Carrasco, and Eric R. Wolf.
New Orleans, Louisiana: Middle American Research Institute,
Tulane University, 1957. 240p. (Publication no. 17).

A collection of four papers on various aspects of Mexican cultural history.

322 **Tijuana: urbanization in a border culture.**
John A. Price. Notre Dame, Indiana: University of Notre Dame
Press, 1973. 108p. maps. bibliog.

A work published under the auspices of the United States-Mexico Border Studies
project of the University of Notre Dame. The book deals with urban development
as influenced by a border culture, and the view of such a culture obtained by
the tourist and the resident.

323 **The truths of others: an essay on nativistic intellectuals in
Mexico.**
Alicja Iwánska. Cambridge, Massachusetts: Schenkman Publish-
ing Co., 1977. 124p. bibliog.

An interesting study of two social movements in Mexico which originated during
the late 1940s; firstly, that of the 'Realists', who believe that the integration of
the Indian population into Mexican society should be done under the leadership
of educated natives born in Indian villages; and secondly, that of the 'Utopians',
who want to transform Mexico into a modern Aztec Empire.

Social Change

324 **Continuity and change in Morelos, Mexico.**
Peter Gerhard. *Geographical Review*, vol. 65, no. 3 (July 1975), p. 335-63.
Traces the changes in political and ecclesiastical divisons since the conquest.

325 **The future of Mexico.**
Edited by Lawrence Koslow. Tempe, Arizona: Arizona State University, Center for Latin American Studies, 1978. 241p. bibliog.
A series of papers presented at a conference entitled 'The Future of Mexico' held at the Center for Latin American Studies, Arizona State University, Tempe, Arizona, April 23-24, 1976. The papers are arranged under the subjects of economics, politics, demography, and international relations.

326 **Growth, equality, and the Mexican experience.**
Morris Singer. Austin, Texas: University of Texas Press, 1969. 341p. bibliog. (Latin American Monographs, 16).
Discusses the relationship betwen social and economic development in Mexico in the 1960s.

327 **In the shadow of Tleloc: life in a Mexican village.**
Gregory G. Reck. New York: Penguin Books, 1978. 224p.
Using one individual as the focus for his book, the author describes changes that have taken place in a remote Mexican village during the mid-1960s with the advent of modernization and a more competitive approach to life. He discusses the differences between the *indio* (native Indian) and *mestizo* (mixed Indian and Spanish ancestry) cultures.

328 **Industrialization in Mexico: old villages and a new town.**
Frank Charles Miller. Menlo Park, California: Cummings Publishing Co., 1973. 161p. maps. bibliog. (The Kiste and Ogan Social Change Series in Anthropology).
A study of the effects of a planned industrial city on traditional small villages surrounding it. Among the factors examined are demographic patterns, standards of living, educational goals, etc.

Social change

329 **Life in a Mexican village: Tepoztlán restudied.**
Oscar Lewis. Urbana, Illinois: University of Illinois Press, 1963.
512p. maps. bibliog.

Another of the author's excellent anthropological studies, this book presents a
second look at Tepoztlán, a Mexican village first studied twenty years earlier by
the anthropologist Robert Redfield.

330 **Nine Mayan women: a village faces change.**
Mary Elmendorf. Cambridge, Massachusetts: Schenkman
Publishing Co., 1976. 159p.

The author presents profiles of nine Mayan women in the Mexican community of
Chan Kom, to show the influence of 'progress' and 'traditionalism' on their lives.

331 **The *rancheros* of Pisaflores: the history of a peasant
bourgeoisie in twentieth-century Mexico.**
Frans J. Schryer. Toronto: University of Toronto, 1980.
210p. bibliog.

A study of the role of the *rancheros* (rural bourgeoisie) in the small town of Pisaflores before, during and after the Mexican Revolution of 1910. A good study of
the plight of landless rural workers, useful to advanced students of Mexico.

332 **Tzintzuntzan: Mexican peasants in a changing world.**
George McClelland Foster. New York: Elsevier-New York, 1979.
392p. bibliog.

An updated study of field work which was originally done between 1945 and
1946, and again between 1958 and 1965. The author records those changes which
took place in the village between 1966 and 1979, and discusses traditional customs
and values which have survived modernization of the society.

Immigration and Emigration

333 **A descriptive study of the control of illegal Mexican migration in the southwestern United States.**
William T. Toney. San Francisco: R & E Research Associates, 1977. 118p. maps. bibliog.
An analytical study of the problem, making use of statistical tables and graphs.

334 **Foreign immigrants in early Bourbon Mexico, 1700-1760.**
Charles F. Nunn. Cambridge, England: Cambridge University Press, 1979. 243p. bibliog. (Cambridge Latin American Studies, 31).
A study of the composition of foreign immigrants to colonial Mexico (soldiers, sailors, merchants, prisoners of war who stayed on, churchmen, etc.), the official attitudes of the government to them, laws that evolved, and the hurdles to acceptance which they faced.

335 **The golden door: international migration, Mexico and the United States.**
Paul R. Ehrlich, Loy Bilderback and Anne H. Ehrlich. New York: Ballantine Books, 1979. 402p. bibliog.
A timely addition to any library on the subject of Mexican-American relations in regard to the problems of migration, 'illegal' immigration, etc.

336 **Mexican immigration to the United States: a study of human migration and adjustment.**
Manuel Gamio. New York: Dover, 1971. 262p. bibliog.
A reprint of a work researched during 1926 and 1927 which studies the history of early large-scale immigration into the United States from Mexico. This work is especially valuable for its documentation of migration from 1918 to 1930 which resulted from the demand for labour during World War I.

337 **Migration and adaptation: Tzintzuntzan peasants in Mexico City.**
Robert V. Kemper. Beverly Hills, California: Sage Publications, 1977. 223p. maps. bibliog. (Sage Library of Social Research, vol. 43).

Based upon field work which took place between 1969 and 1976, this study focuses on the migration and adaptation process which leads from peasant village life to the urban setting of Mexico City.

Politics

338 **Agrarian radicalism in Veracruz, 1930-38.**
Heather Fowler Salamini. Lincoln, Nebraska: University of
Nebraska Press, 1978. 239p. maps. bibliog.
A study of the Veracruz agrarian movement during the 1920s and 1930s under
Tejeda. The author analyses the factors involved in the organization of the
peasants for the creation of a socialist state.

339 **The alienated 'loyal' opposition: Mexico's Partido Acción
Nacional.**
Franz A. Von Sauer. Albuquerque, New Mexico: University
of New Mexico Press, 1974. 197p. bibliog.
A comprehensive work on Mexico's political party, Partido Acción Nacional
(PAN), and its role in Mexican politics.

340 **Authoritarianism in Mexico.**
Edited by José Luis Reyna and Richard S. Weinert. Philadelphia,
Pennsylvania: Institute for the Study of Human Issues, Univer-
sity City Science Center, 1977. 241p. (Inter-American Politics
Series, vol. 2).
A group of essays by United States and Mexican scholars analysing the state
structure of Mexico from the point of view of bureaucracy and authoritarianism.

341 **Azuela and the Mexican underdog.**
Stanley Linn Robe. Berkeley, California: University of
California Press, 1979. 233p. bibliog. (UCLA Latin American
Studies, vol. 48).
The author analyses the background that prompted Azuela's work *Los de abajo*,
of which he includes both Spanish text and English translation.

342 **Benito Juárez.**
Ivie E. Cadenhead. New York: Twayne, 1973. 199p. bibliog.
A brief biography of Juárez, a president of Mexico, concentrating on the years
1855 to 1872, and providing a good political history of the period.

Politics

343 **Democracy in Mexico.**
Pablo González Casanova, translated from the Spanish by
Danielle Salti. New York: Oxford University Press, 1970.
2nd ed. 245p. bibliog.

A translation of the Spanish edition which appeared in 1965 under the title
La Democracia en México, this work examines Mexico's political and social
system, beginning with 1910 and including material gathered up to the 1960s.

344 **Huerta: a political portrait.**
Michael C. Meyer. Lincoln, Nebraska: University of Nebraska
Press, 1972. 272p. bibliog.

A portrait of the régime of Victoriano Huerta from 1913 to 1914 written as a
political biography rather than as a history or as a personal biography.

345 **The impact of revolution: a comparative analysis of Mexico
and Bolivia.**
Susan Eckstein. London; Beverly Hills, California: Sage
Publications, 1976. 55p. bibliog. (Sage Professional Papers in
Contemporary Political Sociology Series no. 06-016, vol. 2).

A study that attempts to analyse comparatively the consequences of two capi-
talist revolutions, those of Mexico and Bolivia.

346 **Intellectual precursors of the Mexican Revolution, 1900-1913.**
James D. Cockcroft. Austin, Texas: University of Texas Press
for the Institute of Latin American Studies, 1968. 329p. maps.
bibliog. (University of Texas. Institute of Latin American Studies.
Latin American Monographs, no. 14).

A scholarly study of the political roles of six Mexican leaders which makes use of
much source material such as newspapers and pamphlets, as well as interviews.

347 **Juárez and Díaz: machine politics in Mexico.**
Laurens Ballard Perry. De Kalb, Illinois: Northern Illinois
University Press, 1978. 467p. maps. bibliog. (Origins of Modern
Mexico).

A thorough analysis of the Mexican political system between 1867 and 1876.
A wealth of material is contained in the many appendices.

348 **Mexican foreign policy under Echaverría.**
Yoram Shapiro. Beverly Hills, California: Sage Publications,
for the Center for Strategic and International Studies, George-
town University, 1978. 84p. bibliog. (Washington Papers, vol. 6,
no. 56). (Sage Policy Paper).

A study of the relationship between President Echeverría's domestic policies and
his foreign policies following the upheavals in Mexico in 1968.

349 **Mexican liberalism in the age of Mora, 1821-1853.**
Charles Adams Hale. New Haven, Connecticut: Yale University
Press, 1968. 347p. bibliog. (Caribbean Series, 11).
A scholarly work which assesses the writings of early 19th century liberals in
Mexico, especially those of José María Luis Mora.

350 **Mexican political biographies, 1935-1975.**
Roderic A. Camp. Tucson, Arizona: University of Arizona
Press, 1976. 468p. bibliog.
Includes biographies of people prominent in Mexican political life between 1935
and early 1974. The appendix contains lists of senators, governors, party execu-
tives, Supreme Court justices, etc.

351 **The Mexican political system.**
Leon Vincent Padgett. Boston, Massachusetts: Houghton
Mifflin, 1976. 2nd ed. 332p. map. bibliog. (Contemporary
Government Series).
A revised version of a work which first appeared in 1966 and which seeks to
analyse the Mexican political system of the present day, while providing some
historical background to changes which have occurred.

352 **The Mexican profit-sharing decision: politics in an authoritarian
regime.**
Susan Kaufman Purcell. Berkeley, California: University of
California Press, 1975. 216p. bibliog.
A case study of the decision-making process at the national level in Mexico. The
author studies the authoritarian aspect of the Mexican political system.

353 **The Mexican reform, 1855-1876: a study in liberal nation-
building.**
Richard N. Sinkin. Austin, Texas: Institute of Latin American
Studies, University of Texas at Austin, 1979. 263p. bibliog.
(Latin American Monographs, no. 49).
A scholarly study of political reform in Mexico between 1855 and 1876. Included
are appendices providing biographical information on reform leaders as well as roll
call votes on key issues.

354 **Mexico in crisis.**
Judith Adler Hellman. New York: Holmes & Meier, 1977. 229p.
bibliog.
One of the few studies on contemporary Mexico which evaluates the country's
economic development and the politics which surround the question of reforms.
This author begins with the Revolution of 1910 and continues to the present day.

Politics

355　Mexico's Acción Nacional: a Catholic alternative to revolution.
Donald J. Mabry. Syracuse, New York: Syracuse University
Press, 1973. 269p. bibliog.

A study of Partido Acción Nacional (PAN), which was formed in 1939 and which
has as its ideology Christian Democracy/Socialism. A good political history.

356　Mexico's leaders: their education and recruitment.
Roderic A. Camp. Tucson, Arizona: University of Arizona
Press, 1980. 259p. bibliog.

A study of the relationship between education and other cultural factors and the
recruitment of Mexico's political leaders between 1911 and the 1950s. The book
is well documented and contains much useful data.

357　Politics and privilege in a Mexican city.
Richard R. Fagen and William S. Tuohy. Stanford, California:
Stanford University Press, 1972. 209p. (Stanford Studies in
Comparative Politics, 5).

The authors study the city of Jalapa, Mexico and base their work on interviews
with citizens, especially members of the élite.

358　Politics and society in Mexico.
Martin C. Needler. Albuquerque, New Mexico: University of
New Mexico Press, 1971. 143p. bibliog.

A work presenting the author's views on Mexican politics during the years
1960-1970.

359　Protest and response in Mexico.
Evelyn Paniagua Stevens. Cambridge, Massachusetts: MIT Press,
1974. 372p. bibliog.

The author describes increasing authoritarianism in Mexican politics, using as case
studies the railway strikes of 1948-59, the doctors' strikes of 1964-65, and the
student strike of 1968.

360　Public opinion in Mexico City about the electoral system.
Kenneth M. Coleman. Chapel Hill, North Carolina: University
of North Carolina Press, 1972. 84p. bibliog. (James Sprunt
Studies in History and Political Science, vol. 53).

An interpretation of a survey taken by the author in Mexico City on the political
system. Included is the text of the questionnaire he used, in both English and
Spanish.

361   **Toncla: conservatism, responsibility, and authority in a Mexican town.**
May N. Diaz.   Berkeley, California: University of California Press, 1966. 234p. bibliog.
A community study dealing with power relationships.

Law and Constitution

362 **Criminal justice in eighteenth century Mexico: a study of the Tribunal of the Acordada.**
Colin M. MacLachlan. Berkeley, California: University of California Press, 1974. 141p. bibliog.
A study of the role of the Tribunal, its functions and eventual decline, in terms of its relation to 18th century notions of criminality and law.

363 **Disorder and progress: bandits, police, and Mexican development.**
Paul J. Vanderwood. Lincoln, Nebraska: University of Nebraska Press, 1981. 264p. bibliog.
A work on 19th century Mexico, focusing on the bandits and *rurales* (policemen) who contributed to the order and disorder of the times.

364 **Judicial review on Mexico: a study of the *amparo* suit.**
Richard Don Baker. Austin, Texas: University of Texas Press for the Institute of Latin American Studies, 1971. 304p. bibliog. (Latin American Monographs, no. 22).
A scholarly study of *amparo* for the use of constitutional defence in legal theory and practice. Cases, established precedents and relevant laws are examined.

365 **Law and social change in Zinacantan.**
Jane Fishburne Collie. Stanford, California: Stanford University Press, 1973. 281p. map. bibliog.
A study of conflict management as influenced by cultural mechanisms of resolution. Such topics as marital disputes, arguments between neighbours, and disputes between an individual and the community, are discussed.

366 **Revolution at Querétaro: the Mexican Constitutional Convention of 1916-1917.**
E. V. Niemeyer. Austin, Texas: University of Texas Press, 1974. 297p. bibliog. (Texas University Institute of Latin American Studies. Latin American Monographs, no. 33).
A discussion of the convention at which Mexico received its present constitution.

367 **A statement of the laws of Mexico in matters affecting business.**
César Sepúlveda. Washington, DC: Pan American Union, 1961.
3rd ed. 268p. bibliog.

A translation of the original Spanish manuscript, which includes material on court organization, domestic relations, nuclear energy, territorial waters, and international agreements.

Administration and Local Government

368 **Bureaucrats, politicians, and peasants in Mexico: a case study in public policy.**
Merilee Serrill Grindle.   Berkeley, California: University of California Press, 1977. 220p. bibliog.

A study of a Mexican agency for rural development under the Echeverría administration (1970-1976). The author uses the technique of the interview to obtain material on policy formation and bureaucratic functioning in such a federal agency in Mexico, and describes the general political environment there.

369 **An empirical analysis of political mobilization: the case of Mexico.**
José Luis Reyna.   New York: Cornell University, Latin American Studies Program, 1971. 213p. bibliog. (Dissertation Series, 26).

A comparative study of Mexican states in politics. Linkages are shown between voter participation and aspects of economic development.

370 **Labyrinths of power: political recruitment in twentieth-century Mexico.**
Peter H. Smith.   Princeton, New Jersey: Princeton University Press, 1979. 384p. bibliog.

A wealth of data is gathered in this volume on more than 6,000 holders of public office in Mexico between 1900 and 1976. The study contributes to our understanding of Mexican politics.

371 **Mexican state government: a prefectural system in action.**
Lawrence S. Graham.   Austin, Texas: Institute of Public Affairs, University of Texas, 1971. 100p. (Public Affairs Series, no. 85).

A case study in state government in Mexico, which uses as its base for field research Morelia, capital city of the state of Michoacán.

372 **Power and conflict in a Mexican community: a study of political integration.**
Antonio Ugalde. Albuquerque, New Mexico: University of New Mexico Press, 1970. 193p. maps. bibliog.

The community of Ensenada, Baja California, is studied and information is given on labour and management organizations, municipal government and politics. Economists would find this work useful for the material on industrial relations and resource allocations.

373 **San Miguel: a Mexican collective** *ejido*.
Raymond Wilkie. Stanford, California: Stanford University Press, 1971. 189p.

Study of the organization (social, economic and political) of a collective *ejido*. The author bases this book on field work carried out in 1953 and in 1966-67, and discusses alternatives to the *ejido*.

Foreign Relations

374   **Arms across the border: United States aid to Juárez during the French intervention in Mexico.**
Robert R. Miller.   Philadelphia, Pennsylvania: American Philosophical Society, 1973. 68p. bibliog. (Transactions of the American Philosophical Society, new series, vol. 63, pt. 6).
A study which is fortified by documents of Juárist agents and the published correspondence of the Mexican minister to the United States.

375   **A century of disagreement: the Chamizal conflict, 1864-1964.**
Sheldon B. Liss.   Washington, DC: University Press, 1965. 167p. maps.
A documented history of the dispute between the United States and Mexico over a tract of land between Ciudad Juárez and El Paso.

376   **Early diplomatic relations between the United States and Mexico.**
William Ray Manning.   New York: Greenwood Press, 1968. 406p. (Albert Shaw Lectures on Diplomatic History, 1913).
A reprint of a 1916 study of diplomatic relations between the United States and Mexico before 1830.

377   **Diplomacy and revolution: U.S.-Mexican relations under Wilson and Carranza.**
Mark T. Gilderhus.   Tucson, Arizona: University of Arizona Press, 1977. 159p. map. bibliog.
A work on the Wilson administration's relations with Carranza, using Mexican and United States archival sources. The author explores Wilson's motivations for his actions.

378 **The diplomacy of annexation: Texas, Oregon and the Mexican War.**
David M. Fletcher. Columbia, Missouri: University of Missouri Press, 1973. 656p. map. bibliog.

An account of the diplomatic context of the war crises of the 1840s. The author examines the role of the Polk administration in the Mexican War and the negotiations surrounding it.

379 **The diplomacy of the Mexican Empire, 1863-1967.**
Arnold Blumberg. Philadelphia, Pennsylvania: American Philosophical Society, 1971. 152p. bibliog. (Transactions of the American Philosophical Society, new series, vol. 61, pt. 8).

A work which seeks to develop the subject of Emperor Maximilian's goals and the role that European statesmen assigned to this French venture in their own political aims.

380 **Dollars over dominion: the triumph of liberalism in Mexican-United States relations, 1861-1867.**
Thomas David Schoonover. Baton Rouge, Louisiana: Louisiana State University Press, 1978. 316p. bibliog.

A book for the specialist in the field of diplomatic history and the politics of 19th century Mexico.

381 **Emissaries to a revolution: Woodrow Wilson's executive agents in Mexico.**
Larry D. Hill. Baton Rouge, Louisiana: Louisiana State University Press, 1973. 394p.

An account of the activities of eleven agents of President Wilson in Mexico, and their influence on his foreign policy and the course of the Mexican Revolution.

382 **The French experience in Mexico, 1821-1861: a history of constant misunderstanding.**
Nancy Nichols Barker. Chapel Hill, North Carolina: University of North Carolina Press, 1979. 264p. bibliog.

An important source of information for students of the period, this work outlines and analyses the relations between France and Mexico during the period from 1821 to 1861.

383 **Great Britain and Mexico in the era of Porfirio Díaz.**
Alfred Paul Tischendorf. Durham, North Carolina: Duke University Press, 1961. 197p. maps. bibliog.

A survey of economic relations between Great Britain and Mexico during the period from 1876 to 1911.

Foreign Relations

384 **The great pursuit.**
Herbert Molloy Mason, Jr. New York: Random House, 1970.
269p. maps. bibliog.
A well-written account of the military expedition undertaken by General John
Pershing into Mexico to capture Pancho Villa. Photographs and maps enhance the
narrative.

385 **Luther T. Ellsworth: U.S. Consul on the border during the
Mexican Revolution.**
Dorothy Pierson Kerig. El Paso, Texas: Texas Western Press,
University of Texas at El Paso, 1975. 80p. map. bibliog.
(Southwestern Studies; Monograph no. 47).
An account of an episode in Mexican history which focuses on the role of a
United States consul, Luther T. Ellsworth, who was first appointed to gather
intelligence at the border. He then was given the task of special respresentative
dealing with neutrality.

386 **The Mexican Revolution, 1910-1914: the diplomacy of Anglo-
American conflict.**
Peter Calvert. London: Cambridge University Press, 1968.
331p. maps. bibliog. (Cambridge Latin American Studies, 3).
Original documents are used to examine events and the relations between British
and American oil companies and diplomats during the time of the Madero and
Huerta governments in Mexico.

387 **Mexico and the Spanish Civil War.**
Thomas G. Powell. Albuquerque, New Mexico: University
of New Mexico Press, 1981. 210p. bibliog.
A new study which draws upon documents, both published and unpublished,
memoirs, newspapers, journals, monographs and interviews, to discuss Mexico's
response to the Spanish Civil War.

388 **Mexico and the United States.**
Jules Archer. New York: Hawthorn Books, 1973. 212p.
bibliog.
A study of relations between the United States and Mexico from colonial to
modern times.

389 **Mexico and the United States, 1821-1973: conflict and
coexistence.**
Karl M. Schmitt. New York: Wiley, 1974. 288p. bibliog.
(America and the World).
A discussion of the interaction between Mexico and the United States, from
the early days of United States territorial expansion to modern times.

390 **Mexico and the United States in the oil controversy, 1917-1942.**
Lorenzo Meyer, translated from the Spanish by Muriel Vascon-
cillos. Austin, Texas: University of Texas Press, 1977. 367p.
bibliog.

A translation of the Spanish work which appeared in 1968. This well-documented
study traces the role of oil in Mexican-United States relations, and discusses the
problems of multinational corporations in developing countries.

391 **Mexico: the quest for a United States policy.**
Peter H. Smith. New York: Foreign Policy Association, 1980.
32p. bibliog.

A publication aimed at clarifying the main issues which are faced by the United
States in its relations with Mexico.

392 **Mexico-United States relations.**
Edited by Susan Kaufman Purcell. New York: Academy of
Political Science, 1981. 213p. (Proceedings of the Academy of
Political Science, vol. 34, no. 1).

A current study which brings up to date the existing literature, discussing such
topics as natural resources (oil, natural gas, etc.), migration, trade relations, etc.

393 **Napoleon III and Mexico: American triumph over monarchy.**
Alfred Jackson Hanna and Kathryn Abbey Hanna. Chapel Hill,
North Carolina: University of North Carolina Press, 1971. 350p.
maps. bibliog.

A well-researched and documented work discussing both French involvement in
Mexico under Napoleon III and United States diplomatic history in Mexico at
the same time.

394 **Pershing's mission in Mexico.**
Haldeen Braddy. El Paso, Texas: Texas Western Press, 1966.
82p.

A short chronological account of Pershing's military pursuit of Villa in Chihuahua.

395 **Prelude to tragedy: the negotiation and breakdown of the
Tripartite Convention of London, October 31, 1861.**
Carl H. Bock. Philadelphia, Pennsylvania: University of
Pennsylvania Press, 1966. 799p. bibliog.

An examination of the background to Maximilian's reign in Mexico – namely the
policies of Britain, France and Spain with regard to Mexico, as well as those of the
United States and Austria.

396 *Revoltosos*: **Mexico's rebels in the United States, 1903-1923.**
W. Dirk Raat. College Station, Texas: Texas A & M University Press, 1981. 394p. bibliog.

A narrative which documents the activities of early groups of Mexican activists operating in the United States during the early 1900s. The influence of these *revoltosos* on the history of both Mexico and the United States is studied.

397 **Revolution and intervention: the diplomacy of Taft and Wilson with Mexico, 1910-1917.**
P. Edward Haley. Cambridge, Massachusetts: M.I.T. Press, 1970. 294p. maps. bibliog.

A study of the roles of the Taft and Wilson administrations in the events in Mexico during the revolutionary civil war period.

398 **Santiago Vidaurri and the Southern Confederacy.**
Ronnie C. Tyler. Austin, Texas: Texas State Historical Association, 1973. 196p. maps. bibliog.

A study of the role played by the man who governed northern Mexico for almost ten years during the 1850s and 1860s, presented against the background of conditions in this Texas-Mexico border area at the time.

399 **The secret war in Mexico: Europe, the United States, and the Mexican Revolution.**
Friedrich Katy. Chicago: University of Chicago Press, 1981. 659p. bibliog.

In 1964 the author published a work entitled *Deutschland, Díaz und die mexikanische Revolution*, which studied German policies in Mexico between 1870 and 1920. In the 1970s, in an attempt to revise this work and to prepare editions in English and Spanish, the author decided to write a completely new book which dealt with the entire interplay of social and diplomatic history in the Mexican Revolution, and was not limited to relations between Mexico and Germany. This book is the result.

400 **The United States and Huerta.**
Kenneth J. Grieb. Lincoln, Nebraska: University of Nebraska Press, 1969. 233p. maps. bibliog.

A study of the role of Woodrow Wilson in intervening in Mexican affairs and in the overthrow of the Huerta régime.

401 **The United States and Mexico.**
James Ford Rippy. New York: AMS Press, 1971. 423p. bibliog.

A reprint of an early survey of diplomatic relations between the United States and Mexico. The period most extensively covered is the thirty years following the Mexican War of 1846-1848.

402 **The United States and Pancho Villa: a study in unconventional diplomacy.**
Clarence Clemens Clendenen. Ithaca, New York: Cornell University Press, 1961. 352p. bibliog.
The author limits his study to the relationship between the United States and Pancho Villa from the beginning of his career to the days of President Wilson.

403 **The United States and revolutionary nationalism in Mexico, 1916-1932.**
Robert Freeman Smith. Chicago: University of Chicago Press, 1972. 288p. bibliog.
An examination of economic relations between the United States and Mexico as a result of Mexican revolutionary nationalism between 1916 and 1929. The author draws on United States and Mexican government archives and the manuscripts of business and political leaders for his wealth of information.

404 **United States-Mexican energy relationships: realities and prospects.**
Edited by Jerry R. Ladman, Deborah J. Baldwin and Elihu Bergman. Lexington, Kentucky: Lexington Books, 1981. 237p. bibliog.
A collection of papers presented at a conference on United States-Mexican energy relationships in December, 1979. The book is divided into four parts dealing with firstly, the background; secondly, the Mexican perspective; thirdly, the United States perspective; and fourthly, the changing conditions of Mexico's external relations – United States, hemispheric, and global.

405 **The United States-Mexico border: a politico-economic profile.**
Raul A. Fernández. Notre Dame, Indiana: University of Notre Dame Press, 1977. 174p. map.
A study of the process of economic change in the border area between Mexico and the United States.

406 **United States-Mexico economic relations.**
Edited by Barry W. Poulson and T. Noel Osborn. Boulder, Colorado: Westview Press, 1979. 442p. (Westview Special Studies in International Economics and Business).
A series of articles which grew out of a symposium participated in by Mexican and United States scholars and dealing with economic problems affecting both nations.

407 **The United States versus Porfirio Díaz.**
Daniel Cosio Villegas.   Lincoln, Nebraska: University of
Nebraska Press, 1963. 259p. bibliog.

A discussion of diplomatic relations between the United States and Mexico during
the Díaz régime.

408 **Views across the border: the United States and Mexico.**
Edited by Stanley R. Ross.   Albuquerque, New Mexico:
University of New Mexico Press, 1978. 456p. map. bibliog.

A series of essays which grew out of a conference sponsored by the Weatherhead
Foundation to study problems relating to the border and frontier zones joining
Mexico and the United States. Among the subjects studied are border culture,
politics, economics, migration, ecology, etc.

409 **Woodrow Wilson and the Mexican Revolution, 1913-1916:**
a history of United States-Mexican relations from the murder of
Madero until Villa's provocation across the border.
Louis M. Teitelbaum.   New York: Exposition Press, 1967. 425p.
maps. bibliog. (Exposition-University Book).

A study of Woodrow Wilson's involvement in Mexican politics and relations
between the United States and Mexico during the Mexican Revolution.

The Economy

410 **Capital formation and economic development in Mexico.**
Joseph S. La Cascia. New York: Praeger, 1969. 190p. bibliog.
(Praeger Special Studies in International Economics and
Development).

A discussion of the role played by capital formation in Mexico during the period
of economic development between 1958 and 1966.

411 **The *despensa* system of food distribution: a case study of
Monterrey, Mexico.**
Stephen H. Gamble. New York: Praeger, 1971. 154p. (Praeger
Special Studies in International Economics and Development).

Discusses a method of food distribution in developing areas. Low-cost staples are
bought by employers at bulk prices and are sold to employees who pay by wage
deductions.

412 **Development of alternatives of Mexico.**
Robert E. Looney. New York: Praeger, 1982. 288p. bibliog.

A recent work which presents economics options which Mexico can follow up to
the end of this century.

413 **The dilemma of Mexico's development: the roles of the private
and public sectors.**
Raymond Vernon. Cambridge, Massachusetts: Harvard
University Press, 1963. 226p.

A study presented by Harvard's Center for International Affairs on the roles of
the government and the private sector in the economic development of Mexico
since 1940.

414 **The economic system of Mexico.**
John B. Ross. Stanford, California: Institute of International
Studies, 1971. 131p. bibliog.

A study of Mexico's economic growth, using 1940 as the base year, and carrying
the study through to 1970.

81

415 The financial development of Mexico.
Raymond W. Goldsmith. Paris: Organization for Economic Co-operation and Development, 1966. 114p.

A survey of the financial structure of the Mexican economy, including many tables of data, and an analysis of those features contributing to Mexico's economic growth.

416 The financial sector and economic development: the Mexican case.
Robert Lee Bennett. Baltimore, Maryland: Johns Hopkins Press, 1965. 210p. bibliog.

A study of post-World War II economic developments in Mexico, as influenced by financial institutions and politics.

417 Inflation, financial markets and economic development: the experience of Mexico.
John K. Thompson. Greenwich, Connecticut: JAI Press, 1979. 239p. bibliog. (Contemporary Studies in Economic and Financial Analysis, vol. 16).

An analysis of Mexican economic development over the last forty years. The author concludes with a chapter discussing options for future growth.

418 Land reform and democracy.
Clarence Senior. Westport, Connecticut: Greenwood Press, 1974. 269p. bibliog.

A reprint of the 1958 edition, this study of the Laguna land reform experiment begun in Mexico in 1936 presents the history preceding the reform, the geography and economic characteristics of the region, and some useful precepts for an agrarian land reform.

419 The Mexican economy: twentieth century structure and growth.
Clark Winston Reynolds. New Haven, Connecticut: Yale University Press, 1970. 468p. map. bibliog.

An analysis of Mexico's economic history and growth, making much use of the interpretation of statistical information.

420 Mexican financial development.
Dwight S. Brothers and Leopoldo M. Solis. Austin, Texas: University of Texas Press, 1966. 236p. bibliog.

This work, which would make an excellent addition to economics collections, describes the Mexican financial system, briefly before 1940, and in greater detail up to 1960.

421 **Mexican monetary policy and economic development.**
B. Griffiths. New York: Praeger, 1972. 174p. (Praeger Special Studies in International Economics and Development).
A work of interest to the specialist in monetary policy and econometrics.

422 **Mexico: mutual adjustment planning.**
Robert Jones Shafer. Syracuse, New York: Syracuse University Press, 1966. 214p. bibliog. (National Planning Series, 4).
A survey of the evolution of economic planning in Mexico.

423 **Mexico's economy: a policy analysis with forecasts to 1990.**
Robert E. Looney. Boulder, Colorado: Westview Press, 1978. 250p. bibliog. (Westview Special Studies on Latin America).
A description of current Mexican economic development and problems.

424 **Mexico's vast economic growth: the Mexican view.**
Austin, Texas: University of Texas Press for the Institute of Latin American Studies, 1967. 217p. (Latin American Monographs, no. 10).
A collection of six essays by Mexican economists on economic growth up to 1964.

425 **Modernization in a Mexican *ejido*: a study in economic adaptation.**
Billie R. De Walt. Cambridge, England; New York: Cambridge University Press, 1979. 303p. bibliog. (Cambridge Latin American Studies, 33).
A scholarly study which shows with the aid of tables and figures the effects of the economic developmental efforts of rural villages in Mexico.

426 **Multilevel planning: case studies in Mexico.**
Edited by Louis M. Goreux and Alan S. Manne. Amsterdam: North-Holland and American Elsevier, 1973. 556p. map.
An important economic study of Mexico, showing the possibilities of planning in the country, using Mexican plans and statistics.

427 **The politics of Mexican development.**
Roger D. Hansen. Baltimore, Maryland: Johns Hopkins Press, 1971. 298p. bibliog.
A study of Mexico's economic development, comparing policies under Porfirio Díaz to the government policies of more recent times.

Economy

428   **Public policy and private enterprise in Mexico.**
Edited by Raymond Vernon. Cambridge, Massachusetts:
Harvard University Press, 1964. 324p. bibliog.

A collection of essays, written by specialists in a readable style, discussing
economic institutions and programmes, and providing the good historical background which is important when studying modern conditions.

429   **Regional economic development: the river basin approach in
Mexico.**
David Barkin and Timothy King. New York: Cambridge
University Press, 1970. 262p. (Cambridge Latin American
Studies, 7).

A review of river basin development in Mexico — primarily the Tepalcatepec River
Basin project — as a means of achieving national development.

430   **The role of economists in policy-making: a comparative case
study of Mexico and the United States.**
Roderic A. Camp. Tucson, Arizona: University of Arizona
Press, 1977. 78p. bibliog. (Institute of Government Research
Publication, University of Arizona).

A comparison of the tactics and influence of economists in Mexico and in the
United States. Two case studies are analysed — the decision of President Kennedy
to reduce income taxes in 1963, and the approval of President Matteo in 1960 of
Mexico's affiliation with the Latin American Free Trade Association.

431   **Scarcity, exploitation, and poverty: Malthus and Marx in Mexico.**
Luis A. Serrón. Norman, Oklahoma: University of Oklahoma
Press, 1980. 279p. maps. bibliog.

A sociologist's analysis of Mexican poverty, with discussion of such aspects as
food, health, housing, mortality, fertility, education, commerce, etc. The author
tests both the Malthusian and Marxist theories in his research.

432   **Socio-economic groups and income distribution in Mexico.**
Wouter van Ginneken. New York: St. Martin's Press, 1980.
237p. bibliog.

A study carried out between 1974 and 1978 by the Income Distribution and
Employment Project of the International Labour Office World Employment
Programme. The author explores the subject of income distribution within the
semi-industrialized country of Mexico, focusing upon aspects of income distribution as reflected by classification according to socio-economic group.

433 Structural change early in development: Mexico's changing
industrial and occupational structure from 1895 to 1950.
Donald B. Keesing. *Journal of Economic History,* vol. 29,
pt. 4 (Dec. 1969), p. 716-38.
Describes long-term trends in Mexico's economic development.

434 Tradition and growth: a study of four Mexican villages.
Manuel Avila. Chicago: University of Chicago Press, 1969.
219p. bibliog.
An interesting study of the villages of Tepoztlán, Mitla, Chan Kom and Sotiapan,
using the comparative method. Earlier anthropological studies are compared by
the author with his later investigations. Unfortunately, as even the author
concedes, the sampling is too small to make generalizations.

435 A village economy: land and people of Huecorio.
Michael Horace Belshaw. New York: Columbia University Press,
1967. 421p. maps. bibliog.
The author, a professor of economics, has studied a Mexican rural village, and
provides much valuable data for the economist and for social scientists in general.

436 Zamora: a regional economy in Mexico.
Oriol Pi-Sunyer. New Orleans, Louisiana: Tulane University,
Middle American Research Institute, 1967. 180p. maps. bibliog.
A study of the relationship of the economy of a provincial town to social and
political factors.

Trade

437 Mexico's foreign trade and economic development.
William O. Freithaler. New York: Praeger, 1968. 160p. bibliog. (Praeger Special Studies in International Economics and Development).

The author discusses Mexico's economic development between 1940 and 1968, especially stressing the successful technique of balancing the importing of essential goods with the border trade and tourism.

438 Politics and trade in Southern Mexico, 1750-1821.
Brian R. Hamnett. New York: Cambridge University Press, 1971. 214p. maps.

An important study of the lucrative dye trade of Oaxaca in the 18th century, in which its economic and political significance are explored.

Business and Industry

439 **The border industrialization program of Mexico.**
Donald W. Baerresen. Lexington, Kentucky: Heath Lexington
Books, 1972. 133p. bibliog.
An examination of a programme which began in 1965, the Border Industrialization
Program, which aimed to provide in Mexico Mexican labour combined with
United States-owned manufacturing operations to supply the United States
market.

440 **Foreign enterprise in Mexico: laws and policies.**
Harry K. Wright. Chapel Hill, North Carolina: University of
North Carolina Press, 1971. 425p.
A review of Mexican government policies since the Revolution which have
affected foreign investment.

441 **Making majolica pottery in modern Mexico.**
Florence C. Lister and Robert H. Lister. *El Palacio*, vol. 78,
pt. 3 (Sept. 1972), p. 21-32.
A description of manufacturing techniques found in Puebla and Guanajicato, and
a history of pottery in Mexico.

442 **Mexican business organizations: history and analysis.**
Robert J. Shafer. Syracuse, New York: Syracuse University
Press, 1973. 397p.
A well-researched work on Mexican business, very useful to those interested in
Mexico's 20th century economic history.

443 **The Mexican mining industry, 1890-1950: a study of the
interaction of politics, economics and technology.**
Marvin D. Bernstein. Albany, New York: State University
of New York Press, 1965. 412p. maps. bibliog.
A detailed scholarly investigation of the Mexican mining industry during the
period covered, including its effects on the country's economy, and government
policy towards the industry.

Business and Industry

444 **Mexican oil and natural gas: political, strategic, and economic implications.**
Richard B. Mancke. New York: Praeger, 1979. 163p. bibliog.
A volume which grew out of a 1978 seminar on international energy and environmental problems at the Fletcher School of Law and Diplomacy.

445 **Mexico: industrialization and trade policies since 1940.**
Timothy King. New York: Oxford University Press, 1970. 160p.
A good study of the economic development of Mexico.

446 **Mexico's oil and gas policy: an analysis.**
US Congressional Research Service. Washington, DC: Government Printing Office, 1979. 67p.
A detailed analysis of Mexico's resources and the likely impact of new finds on United States-Mexican relations.

447 **Miners and merchants in Bourbon Mexico, 1763-1810.**
D. A. Brading. Cambridge, England: Cambridge University Press, 1971. 382p. maps. bibliog. (Cambridge Latin American Studies, 10).
An examination of silver mining and commerce in Bourbon Mexico.

448 **The Mining Guild of New Spain and its Tribunal General, 1770-1821.**
Walter Howe. Cambridge, Massachusetts: Harvard University Press, 1949. 534p. map. bibliog. (Harvard Historical Studies, vol. 56).
A study of the guild which was organized by the mining industry between 1770 and 1820. This was known as the Cuerpo de Minería.

449 **Oil and the Mexican Revolution.**
Merrill Rippy. Leiden, Netherlands: E. J. Brill, 1972. 345p. bibliog.
An english edition of a work originally published in Spanish in 1954 under the title *El petroleo y la revolución Mexicana.* The author studies the struggle during the Mexican Revolution by Mexico to free her oil industry from foreign domination.

450 **The politics of Mexican oil.**
George W. Grayson. Pittsburgh, Pennsylvania: University of Pittsburgh Press, 1980. 283p. maps. bibliog.
A discussion of the Mexican petroleum industry and its role in Mexico's domestic and foreign affairs.

451 **Steel and economic growth in Mexico.**
     William E. Cole.   Austin, Texas: University of Texas Press, 1967.
     173p. bibliog. (Texas University Institute of Latin American
     Studies. Latin American Monograph, no. 7).

A statistical history of the Mexican steel industry and its impact on the rest of the
economy.

Agriculture

452 **Agrarian populism and the Mexican state: the struggle for land in Sonora.**
Steven E. Sanderson.   Berkeley, California: University of California Press, 1981. 290p. bibliog.

Using the state of Sonora as his case study, the author explains the development in Mexico of civil society and the state since independence. He discusses the periods from 1917 to 1940; 1940 to 1970; and finally 1970 to 1976.

453 **Agrarian revolt in a Mexican village.**
Paul Friedrich.   Chicago: University of Chicago Press, 1977. 2nd ed. 162p. maps. bibliog.

An examination of the changes taking place in the southwestern Mexican village of Naranja between 1885 and 1920, which led to an agrarian revolt. The book follows two field projects which were undertaken in 1955-56 and 1966-68. This new edition of the 1970 work contains a new preface and a supplementary bibliography on agrarian reform and local politics.

454 **The agricultural development of Mexico: its structure and growth since 1950.**
Eduardo L. Venezian and William K. Gamble.   New York: Praeger, 1969. 281p. maps. (Praeger Special Studies in Economics and Development).

A survey of the long-term development of Mexican agriculture, analysing farming methods, production, and foreign trade.

455 **Atencingo: the politics of agrarian struggle in a Mexican *ejido*.**
David F. Ronfeldt.   Stanford, California: Stanford University Press, 1973. 283p. bibliog.

A study of agrarian struggle in Atencingo, based upon interviews with peasants in the region, as well as upon government documents, periodical clippings, etc.

90

456 **Campaigns against hunger.**
Elvin Charles Stakman, Richard Bradfield and Paul C.
Mangelsdorf. Cambridge, Massachusetts: Belknap Press of
Harvard University Press, 1967. 328p. maps. bibliog.
A discussion of technical assistance programmes utilized by the Rockefeller
Foundation in order to improve agriculture in Mexico.

457 **Change and uncertainty in a peasant community: the Maya**
corn farmers of Zinacantan.
Frank Cancian. Stanford, California: Stanford University
Press, 1972. 208p. maps. bibliog.
A study of the response of Zinacantan corn-farmers to new roads and a government corn-buying programme. Among aspects discussed are planting practices,
crop yields, marketing arrangements, etc.

458 **Collective farming in northern and southern Yucatán, Mexico:**
ecological and administrative determinants of success and failure.
Jacob Climo. *American Ethnologist*, vol. 5, pt. 2 (May 1978),
p. 191-206.
An excellent study of the comparative implementation of national administrative
policies on communal farms as influenced by local differences in ecology.

459 **Environment and subsistence.**
Edited by Douglas S. Byers. Austin, Texas: University of
Texas Press, 1967. 331p. maps. bibliog. (Prehistory of the
Tehuacán Valley, vol. 1).
Agriculture and the domestication of native American plants are examined in this
volume. Interesting crops found to have been cultivated as early as 5000 B.C.
include maize, avocados and cotton.

460 **The Mexican agrarian revolution.**
Frank Tannenbaum. Hamden, Connecticut: Archon Books,
1968. 543p. bibliog.
An historical view of Mexican land institutions, showing the different approaches
of various peoples to land holding.

Agriculture

461 **Mexican agriculture, 1521-1630: transformation of the mode of production.**
Andre Gunder Frank. Cambridge, England; New York:
Cambridge University Press, 1979. 91p. bibliog. (Studies in
Modern Capitalism).

A work which reflects research undertaken in 1965 and originally written in 1966.
The author intended this study to be the first part of a larger one dealing with the
period from the Conquest to the Revolution, but he never completed the project.
This volume is an analysis of Mexican agriculture immediately following the
Spanish Conquest.

462 **The Mexican *mesa*: the administration of ranching in colonial Mexico.**
William H. Dusenberry. Urbana, Illinois: University of Illinois
Press, 1963. 253p. bibliog.

A useful addition to historical collections, this volume describes the first stock-
men's association in America, and provides documentary information on the
raising of sheep, cattle and horses in colonial Mexico.

463 **Mexico's agricultural dilemma.**
P. Lamartine Yates. Tucson, Arizona: University of Arizona
Press, 1981. 291p. map. bibliog.

An abridged and updated version of a two-volume survey of Mexican agriculture
published in Spanish in 1978 under the title *El Campo Mexicano.*

464 **Modernizing Mexican agriculture: socio-economic implications of technological change, 1940-1970.**
Cynthia Hewitt de Alcantara. Geneva: United Nations Research
Institute for Social Development, 1976. 350p. bibliog. (UNRISD
Studies on the Green Revolution, 11. Report, 76.5).

A well-documented study of agricultural modernization in Mexico, seen as the
result of private and governmental efforts.

465 **Pre-Hispanic Maya agriculture.**
Edited by Peter D. Harrison and B. L. Turner, II. Albuquerque,
New Mexico: University of New Mexico Press, 1978. 414p.
bibliog.

A study which grew out of a symposium held in Paris in 1976 on pre-Hispanic
Maya agriculture.

Transport

466   **Origins of colonial transportation in Mexico.**
       Peter W. Rees. *Geographical Review*, vol. 65, pt. 3 (July 1975),
          p. 323-34.
A discussion of the establishment of transportation routes between Mexico City
and Vera Cruz by the Spaniards, which persist as patterns even today.

467   **The railways of Mexico: a study of nationalization.**
       John H. McNeely. El Paso, Texas: Texas Western College, 1964.
       56p. bibliog. (Southwestern Studies, Monograph 5).
A review of national railway policies from the 19th century to the present.

Labour Movement and Trade Unions

468 **Labor and the ambivalent revolutionaries: Mexico, 1911-1923.**
Ramón Eduardo Ruiz. Baltimore, Maryland: Johns Hopkins
University Press, 1976. 145p. bibliog.

A collection of essays on the development of the labour movement and its
relations with Mexican political leaders during and immediately following the
Mexican Revolution.

469 **Labor organizations in the United States and Mexico: a history of
their relations.**
Harvey A. Levenstein. Westport, Connecticut: Greenwood Press,
1971. 258p.

A scholarly study of the subject.

470 **Organized labor and the Mexican Revolution under Lázaro
Cárdenas.**
Joe C. Ashby. Chapel Hill, North Carolina: University of North
Carolina Press, 1967. 350p. bibliog.

A scholarly work on the growth of the Mexican labour movement during the
period described. The government's role in utilizing labour unions is discussed.

471 **Outcasts in their own land: Mexican industrial workers,
1906-1911.**
Rodney D. Anderson. De Kalb, Illinois: Northern Illinois
University Press, 1976. 407p. maps. bibliog.

A well-researched and documented book on the role of labour in the early 20th
century social upheaval in Mexico. The author's conclusions disagree with some
of those reached in James Cockcroft's *Intellectual precursors of the Mexican
Revolution, 1900-1913.*

472 The political, economic and labour climate in Mexico.
James L. Schlagheck. Philadelphia, Pennsylvania: Industrial
Research Unit, Wharton School, University of Pennsylvania,
1980. 186p. map. (Latin American Studies). (Multinational
Industrial Relations, Series no. 4. Latin American Studies, 4b
— Mexico).

One of a series of books dealing with labour relations in various countries. Other
studies undertaken in this series have covered Australia, Canada, Great Britain,
Peru, Venezuela and Colombia.

Statistics

473 **The aboriginal population of central Mexico on the eve of the Spanish conquest.**
Woodrow Wilson Borah and Sherburne F. Cook. Berkeley, California: University of California Press, 1963. 157p. maps. bibliog. (Ibero-Americana, 45).

A statistical study of the Indian population in Mexico before the arrival of the Spanish. Included in the supporting evidence are tribute materials that became available to the authors.

474 **The Mexican Revolution: federal expenditure and social change since 1910.**
James Wallace Wilkie. Berkeley, California: University of California Press, 1967. 337p. maps. bibliog.

An examination of social change in Mexico resulting from the Mexican Revolution, on the basis of the statistical analysis of federal expenditures.

475 **Mexico: revolution to evolution, 1940-1960.**
Howard Francis Cline. London, New York: Oxford University Press, 1962. 375p. maps. bibliog.

A study of Mexico which includes a wealth of statistical information and much primary source material.

Environment

476   **Environmental problems of the borderland.**
Howard G. Applegate.   El Paso, Texas: Texas Western Press,
1979. 124p. bibliog. (Inter-American Studies, 2).
Increasing attention is being given to the environmental problems of border
areas. This study focuses on the area along the United States-Mexico border.

477   **Fields of the Tzotzil: the ecological bases of tradition in highland
Chiapas.**
George Allen Collier.   Austin, Texas: University of Texas Press,
1975. 255p. maps. bibliog. (Texas Pan-American Series).
An analysis of the traditional life style of the inhabitants of southeastern Mexico,
the Tzotzil tribes, and how this is influenced by the environment, both physio-
graphic and political.

478   **Pollution and international boundaries: United States-Mexican
environmental problems.**
Edited by Albert E. Utton.   Albuquerque, New Mexico:
University of New Mexico Press, 1973. 135p. map. bibliog.
A collection of articles dealing with problems shared by the United States and
Mexico relating to water and air quality as affected by land use.

479   **Prehistoric coastal adaptations: the economy and ecology of
maritime middle America.**
Edited by Barbara L. Stark and Barbara Voorhies.   New York:
Academic Press, 1978. 313p. bibliog. (Studies in Archaeology).
Included in this scholarly volume on the ecology and economy of ancient Middle
American coastal peoples are a number of valuable chapters on areas of Mexico
(e.g. Chiapas, the Southern Isthmus of Tehuantapec, and Southern Veracruz).

Environment

480   **The use of land and water resources in the past and present Valley of Oaxaca, Mexico. Vol. 1: Prehistory and human ecology at the Valley of Oaxaca.**
Anne V. T. Kirkby.   Ann Arbor, Michigan: University of Michigan, 1973. 174p. map. bibliog. (Memoirs of the Museum of Anthropology, 5).

A model is presented for prehispanic developmental stages between 1300 B.C. and A.D. 900. A Spanish summary and appendices are included.

481   **The Valley of Mexico: studies in pre-Hispanic ecology and society.**
Edited by Eric R. Wolf.   Albuquerque, New Mexico: University of New Mexico Press, 1976. 337p. maps. bibliog. (School of American Research Book).

A collection of papers based on a seminar held in Santa Fe, New Mexico, 3-8 April, 1972. They provide a modern view of society in the Valley of Mexico, as shown through archaeological data. The information presented on the ecology of the region is important.

Education

482   **Bureaucracy and national planning: a sociological case study in Mexico.**
Guy Benveniste. New York: Praeger, 1979. 141p. bibliog.
(Praeger Special Studies in International Economics and Development).
A discussion of educational planning in Mexico, centred on the design of the Eleven Year Plan.

483   **Education and national development in Mexico.**
Charles Nash Myers. Princeton, New Jersey: Industrial Relations Section, Dept. of Economics, Princeton University, 1965. 147p. bibliog. (Princeton University. Industrial Relations Section. Research Report Series, no. 106).
A study which shows the correlation of economic growth with education, and which can be compared to findings in other developing nations. The author shows that there is a regional relationship between educational level and the development of the area.

484   **Education and youth employment in less developed countries.**
Berkeley, California: Carnegie Council on Policy Studies in Higher Education, 1978. 115p. bibliog. (Education and Youth Employment in Contemporary Societies).
Part I of the work deals with the education and employment of youth in Mexico. Statistics and projections for the future are included.

485   **Education in a changing Mexico.**
Clark C. Gill. Washington, DC: U.S. Office of Education, Institute of International Studies, 1969. 127p. bibliog.
One of a series of Office of Education publications on education in foreign countries, which covers Mexico's educational aims and achievements between 1959 and 1970.

Education

486 **Higher education in Mexico.**
Thomas Osborn. El Paso, Texas: Texas Western Press, 1976.
150p. map. bibliog.

A history and description of the Mexican higher education system.

487 **Mexico: the challenge of poverty and illiteracy.**
Ramón Eduardo Ruiz. San Marino, California: Huntington
Library, 1963. 234p. bibliog. (Huntington Library Publications).

A good history of education in Mexico, covering the period from 1910 to the
early 1960s. The author attempts to show the role of rural education in an under-
developed nation.

488 **Systems of higher education: Mexico.**
Alfonso Rangel Guerra. New York: Interbook, 1978. 84p.
bibliog. (Systems of Higher Education).

A report on higher education in Mexico which was submitted as part of a comparative study of the subject in twelve countries. This work contains a brief
historical account, followed by material on growth and organization, management or administration, and lastly an analysis of the system's effectiveness.

489 **The University of Mexico and the Revolution: 1910-1940.**
Michael E. Burke. *The Americas*, vol. 34, pt. 2 (Oct. 1977),
p. 252-73.

A description of the interaction between the University of Mexico and revolutionary administrations.

Science and Technology

490   Arithmetic in Maya numerals.
W. French Anderson. *American Antiquity*, vol. 36, pt. 1
(Jan. 1971), p. 54-63.

An analysis of the Mayan numerical system, showing that it could handle
such operations as multiplication, division and square root extraction. The
system is compared with Old World systems.

491   Medicine in Mexico, from Aztec herbs to betatrons.
Gordon Schendel. Austin, Texas: University of Texas
Press, 1968. 329p. bibliog. (Texas Pan-American Series).

An interesting survey of medicine in Mexico, including material on Aztec
medicine, Spanish Colonial medicine, and emphasizing modern Mexican
medicine. The book is intended for medical doctors as well as for the general
public.

492   Skywatchers of ancient Mexico.
Anthony F. Aveni. Austin, Texas: University of Texas Press,
1980. 355p. bibliog. (Texas Pan-American Series).

A useful book for astronomers and also archaeologists, this work shows the
development by Maya and other early Mexican and Central American cultures of
astronomical concepts relating to agriculture, astrology and religion. Many appendices are included, containing useful information such as terms and dates.

**493   Spanish scientists in the New World: the eighteenth-century
expeditions.**
Iris Wilson Engstrand. Seattle, Washington: University of
Washington Press, 1981. 220p. maps. bibliog.

Included in this work on Spanish naturalists in the New World during the late
18th century is much useful information on the establishment of a Royal
Botanical Garden in Mexico City. Also described are the visits of scientists from
two expeditions to Mexico among other ports of call. A number of photographs
and appendices are also included.

Literature

494 After the storm: landmarks of the modern Mexican novel.
Joseph Sommers. Albuquerque, New Mexico: University of
New Mexico Press, 1968. 208p. bibliog.

An analytical work, discussing the novels of Yañez, Juan Rulfo, and Carlos
Fuentes. The works chosen for analysis were written during the period between
1947 and 1962, and will be of interest to the student of Mexican literature.

495 Anthology of Mexican poetry.
Octavio Paz, translated from the Spanish by Samuel Beckett.
London: Thames and Hudson, 1958. 213p. (UNESCO
Collection of Representative Works: Latin American Series).

The selections chosen for translation include material by thirty-five poets who
wrote between 1521 and 1910. Unfortunately, the original Spanish from which
the poems were translated is not included.

496 The *caudillo*: a study in Latin American dictatorships.
Edwin Hemingway Pleasant. Monmouth, Illinois: Commercial
Art Press, 1959. 143p. bibliog.

A literary study of the way in which the *caudillo* is interpreted in various Mexican
revolutionary novels written between 1910 and 1937.

497 Efrén Hernández: a poet discovered.
Mary Harmon. Jackson, Mississippi: University Press of
Mississippi, 1972. 128p. bibliog.

A critical study of the work of Hernández, presented through biographical information as well as statements from the writer and examples from his works
(poetry, novels and stories).

498 **Émilio Carballido.**
Margaret-Sayers Peden. Boston, Massachusetts: Twayne, 1980.
192p. bibliog. (Twayne's World Authors Series, 561: Mexico).
A volume in a series aimed at making world literature available to the English-speaking reader. The author analyses the works of one of Mexico's most famous living dramatists, as well as giving some biographical background and translating some quotations into English.

499 **Fantasy and imagination in the Mexican narrative.**
Ross Larson. Tempe, Arizona: Center for Latin American
Studies, Arizona State University, 1977. 154p. bibliog.
A comprehensive survey of Mexican prose fiction dealing with fantasy and imagination.

500 **Fire and ice: the poetry of Xavier Villaurrutia.**
Merlin H. Forster. Chapel Hill, North Carolina: University of
North Carolina, Department of Romance Languages, 1976. 176p.
(North Carolina Studies in the Romance Languages and Litera-
ture. Essays, 11).
A study of a well-known Mexican poet.

501 **History of Mexican literature.**
Carlos González Peña, translated from the Spanish by Gusta
Barfield Nance and Florence Johnson Dunstan. Dallas, Texas:
Southern Methodist University Press, 1968. 3rd ed. 540p.
An authoritative work on the subject, with critical evaluations of the authors in
the various media – poetry, drama, and the novel – from the 16th to the 20th
centuries.

502 **The Mexican cult of death in myth and literature.**
Barbara L. C. Brodman. Gainesville, Florida: University Press
of Florida, 1976. 89p. bibliog. (University of Florida Monographs.
Humanities Series, 44).
A study tracing the background of the death cult of Aztec and Spanish culture in
the poetry of those cultures. Its presence is shown in the work of five contemporary writers.

503 **The Mexican historical novel, 1826-1910.**
John Lloyd Read. New York: Russell and Russell, 1973. 337p.
bibliog.
A reprint of the 1929 edition published by the Instituto de las Españas en los
Estados Unidos, New York, this work deals with the early Romantic novels
dealing with the Conquest period and the period immediately following, and also
those dealing with the 19th century, which were written by authors living at that
time, and as such were contemporary history.

504 **The Mexican novel comes of age.**
Walter M. Langford. Notre Dame, Indiana: University of Notre
Dame Press, 1971. 229p. bibliog.

A study of Mexican novelists of the 20th century, following a short discussion of
the 19th century novel. This work will be of value to anyone in the field seeking
biographical and literary facts.

505 **Mexican society during the Revolution: a literary approach.**
John David Rutherford. Oxford, England: Clarendon Press,
1971. 347p. bibliog.

The author presents a social history of the Mexican Revolution in which he uses
the novel as his main source of information.

506 **Mexico in its novel: a nation's search for identity.**
John Stubbs Brushwood. Austin, Texas: University of Texas
Press, 1966. 292p. bibliog. (Texas Pan-American Series).

A survey of the novel in Mexican literature from 1521 to 1963, beginning with
the more modern novels and going back in time to the Conquest, and then moving
forward again.

507 **The muse in Mexico: a mid-century miscellany.**
Edited by Thomas Mabry Cranfill. Austin, Texas: University
of Texas Press, 1964. 117p. Supplement to the *Texas Quarterly*,
vol. II, no. 1.

A collection of samples of works in the various arts in mid-20th century Mexico.
Included are works of poetry, fiction and a selection of drawings.

508 **New poetry of Mexico.**
Compiled by Octavio Paz, edited by Mark Strand. New York:
Dutton, 1970. 224p.

A collection of seventy-one poems based on *Poesía en Movimiento, Mexico, 1915-
1966,* published in Mexico in 1966. The works of twenty-four poets are included,
and the translations and brief biographical notes serve to introduce the English-
speaking reader to the field of Mexican poetry.

509 **Octavio Paz: homage to the poet.**
Edited by Kosrof Chantikian. San Francisco: Kosmos, 1981.
248p. bibliog.

A collection of criticism of the work of a renowned Mexican poet and literary
theorist. Also included are a translation of a 1956 play, *Rappaccini's Daughter*,
and several poems.

Literature

510 **Pre-Columbian literature of Mexico.**
Miguel Léon-Portilla, translated from the Spanish by Grace
Lobanov and the author. Norman, Oklahoma: University of
Oklahoma Press, 1969. 191p. bibliog. (Civilization of the
American Indian Series, 92).

A work which presents many examples of pre-Columbian literature (myths, lyric
poetry, early drama, prose, etc.), together with critical comments. The author
attempts to show the symbolism found in the early literature, which includes
examples from Nahuatl, Maya, Mixtec, Zapotec, Tarascan and Otomí literature.

511 **The transformation of the Hummingbird: cultural roots of a
Zinacantecan mythical poem.**
Eva Hunt. Ithaca, New York: Cornell University Press, 1977.
312p. bibliog. (Symbol, Myth, and Ritual Series).

The author provides us with an analysis of the mythical symbolism found in the
poem 'The Hummingbird', and relates it by way of historical records to the
culture in which it originated.

Philosophy

512 **Considerations on the political and social situation of the Mexican Republic, 1847.**
Edited by Dennis E. Berge. El Paso, Texas: Texas Western Press, 1975. 62p. (Southwestern Studies, Monograph no. 45).

A translation of a treatise which was written in Mexico in 1847 as a commentary on the Mexican War. It reveals the division in Mexican society at that time, and is studied by historians interested in the development of liberal ideology in Mexican society.

513 **Major trends in Mexican philosophy.**
Mexico Universidad Nacional Consejo Téchnico de Humanidades. Notre Dame, Indiana: University of Notre Dame Press, 1966. 328p. bibliog.

A collection of seven essays on the history of philosophy in Mexico.

514 **Making of the Mexican mind: a study in recent Mexican thought.**
Patrick Romanell. Lincoln, Nebraska: University of Nebraska Press, 1952. 213p. bibliog.

A book which studies the philosophical history of Mexico, tracing European influences and relating it to Latin American thought.

515 **The modern Mexican essay.**
Edited by José Luis Martínez. Toronto: University of Toronto Press, 1965. 524p. bibliog.

A collection of essays, selected by the editor to reflect a Mexican national outlook and presented in chronological order. The first of the essays was written at the end of the 19th century and the changes in Mexico's social and political history are reflected throughout, while literary and philosophical themes are expressed.

106

516 **Positivism in Mexico.**
Leopoldo Zea. Austin, Texas: University of Texas Press, 1974.
241p. bibliog. (Texas Pan-American Series).
A discussion of the philosophy of positivism in Mexico, which grew with the
Reform movement led by Benito Juárez.

The Arts

General

517 **Art before Columbus: the art of ancient Mexico from the archaic villages of the second millenium B.C. to the splendor of the Aztecs.**
André Emmerich. New York: Simon and Schuster, 1963. 256p. maps. bibliog.

An account which covers ancient Mexican art from the second millenium B.C. to the time of the Aztecs in the 16th century A.D. Many photographs and a glossary of art terms used are included.

518 **The art of ancient Mexico.**
Irmgard Groth-Kimball. London, New York: Thames and Hudson, 1954. 125p.

A beautifully photographed survey with text and notes by Franz Feuchtwanger.

519 **Art of the Huichol Indians.**
Edited by Kathleen Berrin. New York: Abrams for the Fine Arts Museums of San Francisco, 1978. maps. bibliog.

A series of articles on Huichol art forms, written by anthropologists and psychologists, attempting to show these forms from differing points of view. Some present psychological analyses, and others discuss the cultural context of the work.

520 **Arts of ancient Mexico.**
Jacques Soustelle, translated from the French by Elizabeth Carmichael. New York: Viking Press, 1967. 160p. maps. bibliog. (Studio Book).

A view of the arts of early Mexico, including sculpture, pottery, painting, and architecture. The volume includes 206 beautiful photographs taken by Claude Arthaud and F. Hébert-Stevens.

108

521 **Colonial art in Mexico.**
Manuel Toussaint, edited and translated from the Spanish by
Elizabeth Wilder Weismann. Austin, Texas: University of
Texas Press, 1967. 493p. bibliog. (Texas Pan-American Series).
A classic work on Mexican arts and architecture, now available to the English-
speaking reader. Excellent and numerous plates illustrate the book.

522 **A guide to Mexican art, from its beginnings to the present.**
Justino Fernández, translated from the Spanish by Joshua C.
Taylor. Chicago: University of Chicago Press, 1969. 398p.
bibliog.
This illustrated work provides a survey of Mexican art and architecture. The
periods covered are: ancient; the art of New Spain; modern; and contemporary.

523 **Indian art in Middle America.**
Frederick J. Dockstader. Greenwich, Connecticut: New York
Graphic Society, 1964. 221p. maps. bibliog.
Included in this lavishly illustrated work on Indian art in Middle America are
some beautiful Mexican works. The illustrations are accompanied by descriptive
captions.

524 **Indian art of Mexico and Central America.**
Miguel Covarrubias. New York: Knopf, 1957. 360p. maps.
bibliog.
A richly illustrated work on the arts of the early cultures of Mexico and Central
America. The author presents the theories of many schools of archaeology as well
as his own interpretations.

525 **The jaguar's children: pre-classical central Mexico.**
Michael D. Coe. New York: Museum of Primitive Art;
distributed by the New York Graphic Society, Greenwich,
Connecticut, 1965. 126p. maps.
This book is based upon materials assembled for an exhibition of early central
Mexican art which was held at the Museum of Primitive Art from Feb. 17 to
May 5, 1965. About two hundred illustrations from this exhibition are presented,
with descriptive text discussing the Olmec culture.

526 **Master-works of Mexican art, from pre-Columbian times to the
present.**
Fernando Gamboa. Los Angeles: Los Angeles County Museum
of Art, 1964. 296p. maps. bibliog.
The catalogue of a Mexican art exhibition which appeared in many countries over
a period of years. The text provides much material on the ancient Mexican
cultures and their arts, and also included is a comparative chronological chart
covering Europe, the United States and Mexico.

527 **Mexican art.**
Justino Fernández. London: Paul Hamlyn, 1967. 39p. maps. (Colour Library of Art).
A section of fifty-nine beautiful colour plates follows an introductory essay and notes on the plates; these illustrations represent art and architecture covering two thousand years in Mexico.

528 **Mexico.**
Bradley Smith. Garden City, New York: Doubleday, 1968. 296p. bibliog.
A profusely illustrated work which traces Mexican history through its sculpture and painting. Chronologies introducing each era are also included.

529 **Modern Mexican artists: critical notes.**
Carlos Mérida. Freeport, New York: Books for Libraries Press, 1968. 202p. (Essay Index Reprint Series).
A reprint of the 1937 edition, this book presents a series of biographical sketches, with illustrations of the works of the artists included.

530 **Olmec: an early art style of pre-Columbian Mexico.**
Charles R. Wicke. Tucson, Arizona: University of Arizona Press, 1971. 188p. bibliog.
A scholarly work on the Olmec culture, analysing the art from the social and psychological points of view.

531 **Prehispanic Mexican art.**
Paul Westheim and others. New York: Putnam, 1972. 398p. maps. bibliog.
This work, translated from the Spanish, presents many excellent photographs (both in colour and black and white) to illustrate well-known art of the period.

Visual Arts

532 **Ancient sculpture from western Mexico: the evolution of artistic form.**
John L. Alsberg and Rodolfo Petschek. Berkeley, California: Nicole Gallery, 1968. 135p. bibliog.
Critical appraisal of sculpture from Nayarit, Colima and Jalisco, illustrated by very good black and white photographs.

533   **The architecture of Mexico yesterday and today.**
Hans Beacham. New York: Architectural Book Publishing Co.,
1969. 255p.
A collection of excellent black and white photographs of Mexican architecture.
Many building details are included.

534   **The art and architecture of Mexico: from 10,000 B.C. to the
present day.**
Pedro Rojas. London: Hamlyn, 1968. 71p. maps.
A survey of Mexican art and architecture, including a chronological table and a
lavish set of plates with explanatory notes.

535   **Builders in the sun.**
Clive Bamford Smith. New York: Architectural Book Publishing
Co., 1967. 224p.
A well-illustrated volume on the work of Juan O'Gorman, Luis Barragán, Felix
Candelar, Mathias Goeritz and Mario Pani.

536   **The ceramic history of the central highlands of Chiapas, Mexico.**
T. Patrick Culbert. Provo, Utah: Brigham Young University,
1915. 91p. maps. (New World Archaeological Foundation Paper,
19. Publication, 14).
A description of ceramic types and forms found, together with site data from nine
prehistoric Chiapas sites. The period covered ranges from 300 B.C. to A.D. 1524.

537   **Ceramics.**
Richard S. MacNeish, Frederick A. Peterson and Kent V.
Flannery. Austin, Texas: University of Texas Press, 1970. map.
bibliog. (Prehistory of the Tehuacán Valley, vol. 3).
An important work on the development and distribution of Meso-American
ceramics. Included in the study are the Valleys of Mexico and Oaxaca, the Gulf
Coast and the Maya area.

538   **The churches of Mexico, 1530-1810.**
Joseph Armstrong Baird. Berkeley, California: University of
California Press, 1962. 126p. maps. bibliog.
A valuable addition to collections on Mexican architecture and art, this volume
is well illustrated with photographs and line drawings. The author examines many
churches of the period covered which are not discussed in other works, and illustrates variations in regional architecture.

539 **Colossal heads of the Olmec culture.**
C. William Clewlow, Richard A. Cowan, James F. O'Connell and
Carlos Benemann. Berkeley, California: University of California,
Archaeological Research Facility, 1967. 170p. maps. bibliog.
(Contribution, 4).

A well-illustrated, detailed volume on twelve stone sculptures in the round. Information is given on style, sculpting techniques employed and the condition of the works.

540 **Crafts of Mexico.**
Marian Harvey. New York: Macmillan, 1973. 243p.

An illustrated volume containing descriptive sections on weaving, reeds, metals, clay, wood and paper.

541 **Design motifs of ancient Mexico.**
Jorge Enciso. New York: Dover, 1953. 153p.

A collection of primitive designs derived from carved stamps made by early Mexican peoples, and now of use to artists, designers, etc. Originally published under the title *Sellos del antiguo México*.

542 **Designs from pre-Columbian Mexico.**
Jorge Enciso. New York: Dover, 1971. 105p. (Dover Pictorial
Archives).

An illustrated collection of three hundred original motifs created by pre-Columbian Mexican peoples such as the Aztecs, Toltecs and others. These designs were found in archaeological digs on malacates, objects of baked clay. A good source for artists, designers and others.

543 **Dominican architecture in sixteenth century Oaxaca.**
Robert J. Mullen. Phoenix, Arizona: Arizona State University,
Center for Latin American Studies, 1975. 260p. bibliog.

A study of over seventy church-convent complexes founded by the Dominicans, giving case histories, architectural styles, foundation dates, etc.

544 **An early stone pectoral from southeastern Mexico.**
Michael D. Coe. Washington, DC: Dumbarton Oaks Trustees
for Harvard University, 1966. 18p. bibliog. (Studies in Pre-
Columbian Art and Archaeology, no. 1).

An examination of a pectoral in the Robert Wood Bliss collection of pre-Columbian art at Dumbarton Oaks.

545 **Edzná, Campeche, Mexico: settlement patterns and monumental architecture.**
George F. Andrews and others. Eugene, Oregon: University of Oregon, Department of Architecture, 1969. 149p. maps.
The most useful data in this work consists of maps, analyses of buildings, site plans, and photographs of stelae and glyph panels which have not been published in other sources.

546 **A guide to architecture in ancient Mexico.**
Paul Gendrop. Mexico City: Editorial Minutiae Mexicana, 1974. 128p. maps. bibliog.
A study of Mesoamerican architecture, including examples of regional styles.

547 **A history of Mexican mural painting.**
Antonio Rodríguez, translated from the Spanish and German by Marina Corby. New York: G. P. Putnam's Sons, 1969. 571p.
An analysis of pre-Columbian art as seen in murals and pottery.

548 **The iconography of the art of Teotihuacán.**
George Kubler. Washington, DC: Dumbarton Oaks Trustees for Harvard University, 1967. 40p. bibliog. (Studies in Pre-Columbian Art and Archaeology, no. 4).
A short study of the iconographic relationships found in Teotihuacán art.

549 **Lords of the underworld: masterpieces of classic Maya ceramics.**
Michael D. Coe. Princeton, New Jersey: Art Museum, Princeton University; distributed by Princeton University Press, 1978. 142p. bibliog.
A profusely illustrated catalogue of ceramics; detailed descriptive text accompanies each photograph. This book formed the catalogue to an exhibition held at the Princeton University Art Museum, 4 March-18 June 1978.

550 **M. Alvarez Bravo.**
Jane Livingston. Boston, Massachusetts: David R. Godine, 1978. 45p.
A collection of photographs which illustrate the work of one of Mexico's best-known photographers. The author provides a text describing the photographer's fifty-year career.

551 **Mexican art and the Academy of San Carlos, 1785-1915.**
Jean Charlot. Austin, Texas: University of Texas Press, 1961.
177p. (Texas Pan-American Series).

An attempt to understand the period of neo-classicism in Mexico, which was dominated by the Royal Academy of San Carlos, founded in 1785 by the king of Spain. This period lies between the colonial and modern periods of Mexican art.

552 **Mexican folk art.**
Gerd Dörner, translated from the German by Gladys Wheelhouse.
Munich, Vienna: W. Andermann Verlag, 1962. 67p. bibliog.

A history of Mexican folk art, with many coloured photographs. Included are examples of pottery, weaving, beadwork, etc.

553 **Mexican interiors.**
Verna Cook Shipway and Warren Shipway. New York:
Architectural Book Publishing Co., 1962. 257p.

A photographic collection of Mexican interiors, illustrating both surviving examples from colonial times and folk art used in restored colonial and modern homes. Details are emphasized, such as tiles, screens, ceramics, fireplaces, gardens, etc.

554 **Mexican landscape architecture: from the street and from within.**
Rosina Greene Kirby. Tucson, Arizona: Arizona University
Press, 1972. 163p. bibliog.

The author makes good use of excellent photographs to illustrate Mexican landscape design. Material on plazas, parks, patios and gardens is included.

555 **Mexican manuscript painting of the early colonial period.**
Donald Robertson. New Haven, Connecticut: Yale University
Press, 1959. 234p. bibliog.

The author studies a group of manuscripts from the Central Valley of Mexico, and traces Spanish influence on Indian styles.

556 **Mexican masks.**
Donald Cordry. Austin, Texas: University of Texas Press, 1980.
280p. maps. bibliog.

A richly illustrated volume covering the subject from the points of view of art, symbolism, history, and psychology of use.

557 **The Mexican muralists.**
Alma M. Reed. New York: Crown, 1960. 191p.

An introduction to mural painting containing biographies of more than thirty Mexican artists who worked in this field, including Orozco, Rivera and Siqueiros.

558 **Mexican painting in our time.**
Bernard S. Myers. New York: Oxford University Press, 1956.
283p. bibliog.

An illustrated history of Mexican painting from 1920 to the 1950s. The author relates the artists' works to the historical period out of which they grew.

559 **Mexican popular arts: being a fond glance at the craftsmen and their handiwork in ceramics, textiles, metals, glass, paint, fibres and other materials.**
Frances Toor. Detroit, Michigan: Blaine Ethridge, 1973. 107p.

An updated reissue of the 1939 work *Mexico*, issued by the Frances Toor Studios. Most of the popular arts and crafts of Mexico are covered in this work.

560 **Mezcala stone sculpture: the human figure.**
Carlos T. E. Gay. Greenwich, Connecticut: New York Graphic Society, 1967. 39p. maps. bibliog. (Museum of Primitive Art. Studies, no. 5).

A study of ancient stone sculpture found in the Mexican state of Guerrero.

561 **The open-air churches of sixteenth-century Mexico: *atrios, posas, open chapels, and other studies.***
John McAndrew. Cambridge, Massachusetts: Harvard University Press, 1965. 755p. bibliog.

A beautiful work of architectural history, which includes line drawings of the structures discussed, and provides a view of 16th century Mexican life.

562 **Painted walls of Mexico: from prehistoric times until today.**
Emily Edwards. Austin, Texas: University of Texas Press, 1966. 306p. maps. bibliog. (Elma Dill Russell Spencer Foundation Series).

An attractive catalogue of hundreds of Mexican wall paintings. The author attempts to give equal coverage to each style and period, and the people and events of the times are briefly discussed.

563 **Pre-Columbian architecture of MesoAmerica.**
Doris Heyden and Paul Gendrop. New York: Abrams, 1976. 340p. (History of World Architecture Series).

A well-illustrated survey of pre-Columbian architectural styles, which focuses on key archaeological sites and discusses the culture of the period.

564 **Pre-Columbian Mexican miniatures: the Josef and Anni Albers collection.**
Anni Albers. New York: Praeger, 1970. 84p. bibliog.

A well-illustrated catalogue of Mesoamerican figurines and other miniature objects, with introductory text and informative captions.

565 **The Puuc: an architectural survey of the hill country of Yucatán and northern Campeche, Mexico.**
Harry Evelyn Dorr Pollock. Cambridge, Massachusetts: Peabody Museum of Archaeology and Ethnology, Harvard University, 1980. 600p. map. bibliog. (Memoirs of the Peabody Museum, vol. 19).

A detailed architectural study of the Mayan works of the Yucatán peninsula, with photographs, architectural renderings, plans, etc. A very useful reference work.

566 **Rock art of Baja, California.**
Campbell Grant. Los Angeles: Dawson's Book Shop, 1974. 146p. maps. bibliog. (Baja California Travels Series, 33).

A beautifully illustrated volume which was based on a translation of Léon Diguet's article of 1895 on rock art of Baja California Sur, and then expanded.

567 **The sculpture of ancient Mexico.**
Paul Westheim, translated from the Spanish by Ursula Bernard. Garden City, New York: Doubleday, 1963. 69p. (Anchor Books, A335).

A paperback volume in which the author discusses pre-Columbian sculpture, and illustrates selected clay and stone objects in a series of ninety-four plates. Originally published in German and translated into Spanish by Mariana Frank.

568 **Sculpture of ancient west Mexico: Nayarit, Jalisco, Colima; the Proctor Stafford collection.**
Los Angeles: Los Angeles County Museum of Art, 1970. 116p. map. bibliog.

The beautifully illustrated catalogue of an exhibition of pottery, figurines, and vessels held 7 July-30 August 1970. Detailed descriptive material is included, together with two articles, one on aesthetics and the other on ceramic mortuary offerings of early west Mexico, and a chronological chart.

569 **The sculpture of El Taj in Veracruz, Mexico.**
Michael Edwin Kampen. Gainesville, Florida: University of Florida Press, 1972. 195p. bibliog.

A study of sculptural techniques, forms, etc., accompanied by a descriptive catalogue containing line drawings.

570 **Some hypotheses regarding the petroglyphs of West Mexico.**
Joseph B. Mountjoy. Carbondale, Illinois: University Museum,
Southern Illinois University at Carbondale, 1974. 36p. maps.
bibliog. (Mesoamerican Studies, no. 9).
A brief study of an art form which has previously received little attention, and
which is compared to designs found in ceramics, textiles, plastered walls, etc.

571 **Stonework of the Maya.**
Edward Ranney. Albuquerque, New Mexico: University of
New Mexico Press, 1974. 119p. bibliog.
A beautiful collection of photographs accompanies the text of this book, which
discusses the stonework of the Maya as part of the natural setting in which it
stands.

572 **Style in Mexican architecture.**
Richard Aldrich. Coral Gables, Florida: University of Miami
Press, 1968. 110p.
A critical text, accompanied by sixty-four very good black and white photographs,
illustrating Mexican architecture from pre-Columbian to modern. Many colonial
examples are given, including numerous churches.

573 **A stylistic and chronological study of Olmec monumental
sculpture.**
Carl William Clewlow, Jr. Berkeley, California: University of
California, Department of Anthropology, 1974. bibliog.
(University of California Archaeological Research Facility.
Contributions, no. 19).
A monograph which presents a slightly revised version of the author's doctoral
dissertation.

Music

574 **Classic Maya music: pt. 1, Maya drama; pt. 2, rattles, shakers,
raspers, wind and string instruments.**
Norman Hammond. *Archaeology*, vol. 25, pt. 2 (April 1972),
p. 124-31; vol. 25, pt. 3 (June 1972), p. 222-28.
Descriptions of various instruments as represented in pictorial and documentary
sources (e.g. sculpture, murals, Maya codices, and Spanish texts).

575 **The Mexican *corrido* as a source for interpretive study of modern Mexico (1870-1950).**
Merle Edwin Simmons. Bloomington, Indiana: Indiana University Press, 1957. 619p. bibliog. (Indiana University Publications. Humanistic Series, no. 38).

A discussion of the Mexican ballad or *corrido* as a source of information about Mexican life from 1870 to the 1950s.

576 **The Mexican *son*.**
E. Thomas Stanford. *Yearbook of the International Folk Music Council* (UNESCO), (1972). p. 66-86.

Information on the types of music known in Mexico as *sones*, including terms related to songs, dances and musical instruments.

577 **Music in Aztec and Inca territory.**
Robert Stevenson. Berkeley, California: University of California Press, 1968. 378p.

An important work containing much of what is known about the music of central Mexico. Most of the material has been gleaned from documentary and native pictorial sources.

578 **Music in Mexico: a historical survey.**
Robert Murrell Stevenson. New York: Crowell, 1952. 300p.

The first scholarly book in English on the history of music in Mexico from Aztec to modern times.

579 **Musical artefacts of pre-Hispanic west Mexico: towards an interdisciplinary approach.**
Peter Crossley-Holland. Los Angeles: Program in Ethnomusicology, Department of Music, University of California, 1980. 45p. bibliog. (Monograph Series in Ethnomusicology, no. 1).

A monograph providing information on musical instruments seen in their cultural setting. They are interpreted using integrated musicological, archaeological and historical data.

Theatre and Film

580 **The Mexican cinema: interviews with thirteen directors.**
Beatriz Reyes Nevares. Albuquerque, New Mexico: University
of New Mexico Press, 1976. 192p.

A study of avant-garde ideas in Mexican cinema, based upon interviews with
noted Mexican film directors.

581 **Mexican theater of the twentieth century: bibliography and
study.**
Ruth S. Lamb. Claremont, California: Ocelot Press, 1975.
2nd ed. 140p.

This useful bibliography includes an introductory essay discussing the theatre in
three stages: 'Emancipation – 1900-1930'; 'Renovation – 1928-1950'; and 'New
Theatre – 1950-1975'. Also presented are a critical bibliography and a list of
periodicals containing threatre criticism, bibliography, and texts of plays.

Folklore

582 **Amapa storytellers.**
Edited by Stanley L. Robe. Berkeley, California: University
of California Press, 1972. 108p. bibliog.

A collection of fifteen orally collected texts gathered in Amapa, Nayarit in 1959.
The tales are briefly summarized in English, and notes give information on other
versions of each tale, and identify tale types. There is an informative introduction
describing the village, its population and tale-telling customs.

583 **The ephemeral and the eternal of Mexican folk art.**
Mexico City: Fondo Editorial de la Plástica Mexicana, 1971.
2 vols. bibliog.

A beautifully illustrated work on Hispanic folklore, with many informative
commentaries by various specialists. The many colour photographs are of special
interest to the folklorist.

584 **Folktales of Mexico.**
Compiled by Americo Paredes. Chicago: University of Chicago
Press, 1970. 282p. bibliog. (Folktales of the World).

An excellent collection of eighty tales, which includes a glossary and indexes of
tale types and motifs.

585 **A guide to Mexican witchcraft.**
William Madsen and Claudia Madsen. Mexico City: Editorial
Minutiae Mexicana, 1972. 96p. bibliog. (Minutiae Mexicana
Series).

A popular account of folk medical practices in early and contemporary Mexico.
The relationship between concern with withcraft and economic mobility is shown
by anecdotes.

586 **Mexican and Central American mythology.**
Irene Nicholson. London: Hamlyn, 1967. 141p. bibliog.

A profusely illustrated book on the mythology of the region.

587 **Mexican folk *retablos*.**
Gloria Kay Giffords. Tucson, Arizona: University of Arizona
Press, 1974. 160p.

A well-illustrated work on Mexican folk paintings of saints.

588 **Mexican folk tales.**
Edited by Anthony John Campos. Tucson, Arizona: University
of Arizona Press, 1977. 136p.

A collection of Chicano legends, translated by the editor into English, and
Mexican in origin, representing rural Jalisco.

589 **Mexican folk tales.**
Juliet Piggott. New York: Crane Russak, 1976. 128p.

This volume contains myths and legends deriving from both the Indian and
Spanish backgrounds of the Mexican people.

590 **Mexican folktales from the borderland.**
Riley Aiken. Dallas, Texas: Southern Methodist University
Press, 1980. 159p.

A collection of stories which the author gathered over a period of years beginning
in 1929, representing the culture of the Mexican-Indian rural borderland.

591 **Mexican folk toys: festival decorations and ritual objects.**
Florence H. Pettit and Robert M. Pettit. New York: Hastings
House, 1978. 185p. bibliog.

An examination of a folk art from the point of view of history and sociology.
Beautiful photographs illustrate a book which contains material on the techniques
and materials used by the craftspeople; a calendar of Mexican festivals and
holidays; and a list of places such as museums and shops where such folk toys and
ritual objects can be found.

592 **Mexican tales and legends from Los Altos.**
Edited by Stanley L. Robe. Berkeley, California: University
of California Press, 1970. 578p. bibliog.

Two hundred and nineteen tales are presented in Spanish with English summaries.
They are identified by tale type and theme. Much information is provided on the
Los Altos region of Jalisco.

593 **Ritual humor in highland Chiapas.**
Victoria Reifler Bricker. Austin, Texas: University of Texas
Press, 1973. 257p. maps. bibliog. (Texas Pan-American Series).

A study of the ritualized humour found in songs, costumes, etc. used during the
Christmas, New Year, Epiphany, and Carnival festivals of Chiapas.

594 **A treasury of Mexican folkways.**
Frances Toor. New York: Crown, 1971. 566p.

An illustrated collection of customs, legends, dances and songs (including music),
fiestas, etc. of the Mexican people.

Costume

595 **Mexican Indian costumes.**
Donald Cordry and Dorothy Cordry. Austin, Texas: University
of Texas Press, 1968. 373p. maps. bibliog.

A beautifully illustrated volume on pre-Hispanic and modern costume. Information on weaving, design, jewellery and much else is included.

596 **Riders of the border: a selection of thirty drawings.**
José Cisneros. El Paso, Texas: Texas Western Press, University
of Texas at El Paso, 1971. 64p. bibliog. (Southwestern Studies,
Monograph no. 30).

One of the few existing collections of renderings showing details of clothing worn
by various people in Mexico and the Spanish southwest of the United States
throughout history. All the types represented in this collection are riders on
horseback, and vary from the 16th century Spanish conquistador to the 20th
century Colima rider.

Food

597 Better homes and gardens Mexican cook book.
Des Moines, Iowa: Meredith, 1977. 96p. (Better Homes and
Gardens Books).
An attractively illustrated cookery book, presenting recipes for Mexican cooking.

598 The complete book of Mexican cooking.
Elizabeth Lambert Ortiz. New York: M. Evans, 1967. 352p.
Three hundred and forty recipes present the blend of influences in Mexican
cookery, combining Aztec, Spanish and French cuisine.

599 The cuisines of Mexico.
Diana Kennedy. New York: Harper and Row, 1972. 378p.
bibliog.
A well-researched book, written by the wife of a New York Times correspondent
who lived for a number of years in Mexico, and gathered recipes from local
kitchens as well as ancient cookery books. There is an introduction by Craig
Claiborne, and appetizing colour photographs of some of the dishes.

600 The food and drink of Mexico.
George C. Booth. Los Angeles: Ward Ritchie Press, 1964.
190p.
A traditional cookery book which contains recipes gathered by the author
throughout his travels in Mexico.

601 Mexican cook book.
Culinary Arts Institute. Chicago: Consolidated Book Publishers,
1976. 96p. (Adventures in Cooking Series).
A collection of recipes adapted for the American cook who wishes to prepare
Mexican meals using standard kitchen appliances.

602   The Mexican cuisine I love.
Jules J. Bond. New York: Leon Amiel, 1977. 160p.

A collection of recipes for traditional dishes of Mexico, based upon both the Spanish influence on Mexican cooking, and the foods taken back to Europe by the Spaniards from Mexico, for instance tomatoes, corn and avocados. Beautiful coloured plates enhance this book.

603   **Recipes from the regional cooks of Mexico.**
Diana Kennedy. New York: Harper and Row, 1978. 288p.

A cookery book which includes local recipes of Mexican dishes as well as anecdotes describing regional customs. The author has won acclaim for her previous books on Mexican cookery.

604   **Savoring Mexico: a travel cookbook.**
Sharon Cadwallader. New York: McGraw-Hill, 1980. 207p.
maps. Paperback edition, McGraw-Hill Paperback Series, 160p.

A sampling of regional cookery throughout Mexico by an author who has chosen recipes that are both representative of the cuisine and easy to prepare outside Mexico.

Museums and
Libraries

605 **The Mexican library.**
Paul Howard Bixler. Metuchen, New Jersey: Scarecrow Press,
1969. 129p.
The author's report on the study undertaken with Dr. Carl M. White emphasizes
those Mexican libraries serving higher education. The author concludes that not
enough support, in terms of both financial backing and personnel training, is
given. Recommendations for improvements are made.

606 **Mexico's library and information services: a study of present
conditions and needs.**
Carl M. White. Totowa, New Jersey: Bedminster Press, 1969.
106p.
This report, the result of a study undertaken with Dr. Paul H. Bixler (see previous
entry), concentrates on Mexico's library needs in terms of the country's national
goals. The author makes recommendations for the future development of
libraries and librarianship in Mexico, emphasizing education, federal assistance,
urbanization, etc.

607 **The National Museum of Anthropology, Mexico: art, architecture,
archaeology, anthropology.**
Pedro Ramirez Vásquez. New York: Abrams, 1968. 257p.
maps. bibliog.
An excellent introductory study of the art and peoples of Mexico, this book
describes the magnificent museum located in Mexico City's Chapultepec Park.
Many photographs are included.

608 **National Museum of Anthropology, Mexico City.**
Carlo Ludovico Ragghianti and Licia Ragghianti Collobi. New
York: Newsweek, 1970. 171p. bibliog. (Great Museums of the
World).
Spectacular colour plates illustrate the textual description of one of the finest
museums in the world.

125

609 **3000 years of art and life in Mexico, as seen in the National Museum of Anthropology, Mexico City.**
Ignacio Bernal, translated from the Spanish by Carolyn B. Czitrom. New York: Abrams, 1968. 216p.

An illustrated description and history of the museum which opened in 1964 and which provides a superb panorama of Mexican life and culture throughout the ages.

610 **Treasures of ancient Mexico from the National Anthropological Museum.**
Maria Antonieta Cervantes. New York: Crescent Books, 1978. 95p.

A series of photographs with descriptive text of the exhibits to be found in Mexico City's National Anthropological Museum. The book is arranged as a study in three parts: pre-Hispanic archaeology, the European Conquest, and ethnography.

The Press

611 Artes de México.
Mexico City: Artes de México y del Mundo, 1953- . bimonthly.
A magazine devoted to the arts. Contains articles written in Spanish with English and sometimes French translations.

612 Artes Visuales.
Mexico City: Museo de Arte Moderno, 1973- . quarterly.
A beautifully illustrated quarterly periodical published by the Museum of Modern Art in Mexico City. The Spanish articles, accompanied by English translations, deal with the arts in Mexico.

613 Excelsior.
Mexico City: Editorial Excelsior S.C.L., 1916- . daily.
A prestigious newspaper covering all features of Mexican life. This leading Spanish-language newspaper covers Latin American as well as world news, and features extensive sports coverage.

614 Hispano Americano: semanario de la vida y la verdad.
Mexico City: Tiempo S.A. de C.V., 1970- .
A Mexican news magazine in Spanish, with a format similar to *Time Magazine*. This title was used from 1970 for United States distribution of the magazine *Tiempo*, which began publication in 1946.

615 Historia Mexicana.
Mexico City: El Colégio de México, 1951- . quarterly.
Written entirely in Spanish, this periodical contains studies on the history of Mexico.

616 Mexican World: the voice of Latin America.
Minneapolis, Minnesota: Graphic Services, Inc., 1966- .
A popular type of magazine, written by and for tourists, providing information for those desiring to travel, study, or retire in Mexico.

617 **Mexico Desconocido.**
Mexico City: Organización Editorial Novaro, 1976- .
Written in Spanish for a Mexican public, with beautiful full colour photographs of Mexico.

618 **Mexico This Month.**
Mexico City: Altenas, 1955- . monthly.
A monthly tourist and business-oriented magazine, suitable for inclusion in a public library.

Reference Works

619 American Chamber of Commerce of Mexico: membership directory.
Mexico City: American Chamber of Commerce of Mexico.
annual.
A listing of Mexican and American businesses interested in trade and investment between the two countries.

620 Anglo-American directory of Mexico.
Mexico City: Monclova, 1932- . annual.
A directory listing names, addresses, business affiliations etc. of Anglo-Americans living in Mexico. Much useful information is given here, including embassy and consulate staffs, emergency telephone numbers, and a classified section.

621 An annotated bibliography of the novels of the Mexican revolution of 1910-1917, in English and Spanish.
John Rutherford. Troy: Whitston, 1972. 180p.
Much useful reference information is found here, including brief essays on the novelists, criticism, editors, etc. The text is provided in both English and Spanish, making it a good reference work for readers of either language.

622 Area handbook for Mexico.
Thomas E. Weil, Jan Knippers Black, Howard I. Blutstein, Kathryn Theresa Johnson and David S. McMorris. Washington, DC: U.S. Government Printing Office, 1975. 2nd ed. 450p. maps. bibliog.
One of a series of handbooks prepared by Foreign Area Studies of the American University. Contains much useful information for personnel such as the military, who might need to know about various aspects of a country, such as the social, political and economic practices.

623 **The art and archaeology of pre-Columbian middle America:**
     an annotated bibliography of works in English.
     Aubyn Kendall. Boston, Massachusetts: G. K. Hall, 1977.
     324p. (Reference Publications in Latin American Studies).

This bibliography covers the area comprising Mexico, Guatemala, El Salvador, Honduras, Belize, Costa Rica, Nicaragua and Panama. Included are the revised entries from the author's earlier work, *The Art of Pre-Columbian Mexico: an Annoted Bibliography of Works in English*, 1973.

624 **The art of pre-Columbian Mexico: an annotated bibliography of**
     works in English.
     Aubyn Kendall. Austin, Texas: Institute of Latin American
     Studies, University of Texas, 1973. 115p. (Guides and Biblio-
     graphic Series, 5).

In addition to the useful annotated bibliography, there is an appendix listing works not yet examined, or received too late to be included in the alphabetical arrangement.

625 **A bibliography of Chicano and Mexican dance, drama and music.**
     Jorge A. Huerta. Oxnard, Mexico: Colégio Quetzalcoatl, 1972.
     59p.

This bibliography, which is in the form of a pamphlet, is divided into three areas: dance, drama and music. Each subject is divided according to pre-Columbian, Mexican and Aztlan peoples. Annotations are not included.

626 **The Harkness Collection in the Library of Congress: manuscripts**
     concerning Mexico, a guide; with selected transcriptions and
     translations by J. Benedict Warren.
     U.S. Library of Congress. Manuscript Division. Washington, DC:
     Library of Congress, 1974. 315p. bibliog.

A guide to a collection of documents presented to the Library of Congress between 1928 and 1929. The Mexican portion of the collection is covered in this volume, and relates to the early history of the Spanish in Mexico.

627 **The historical dictionary of Mexico.**
     Donald C. Briggs and Marvin Alisky. Metuchen, New Jersey:
     Scarecrow Press, 1981. 259p. bibliog. (Latin American Historical
     Dictionaries, no. 21).

A one-volume reference tool providing short entries on various facets of both modern and historical Mexican life.

628 **Index of Mexican folktales, including narrative texts from
Mexico, Central America, and the Hispanic United States.**
Stanley L. Robe. Berkeley, California: University of California
Press, 1973. 276p. bibliog.
A useful index of about fifteen hundred Hispanic-Mexican folktales, classified
according to the Aarne-Thompson system. The index does not include tales of
purely native origin.

629 **An index to Mexican literary periodicals.**
Merlin H. Forster. New York: Scarecrow, 1966. 276p.
Sixteen Mexican literary periodicals are indexed. These publications cover the
period from 1920 to 1960, and most of them are not indexed elsewhere.

630 **The men who made Mexico.**
Clarke Newlon. New York: Dodd, Mead, 1973. 273p. bibliog.
A collection of biographical sketches of Mexican leaders, noting their influence on
Mexican history.

631 **Mexican exports.**
Madero, Mexico: Editora Mexicana de Servicios de Información,
S.A. annual.
An alphabetical list of Mexican companies interested in export.

632 **Mexican literature: a bibliography of secondary sources.**
David William Foster. Metuchen, New Jersey: Scarecrow Press,
1981. 386p.
A bibliography of criticism of major Mexican literary figures. The book is divided
into two parts: General References, and Authors. The compiler states that the
bibliography is selective, depending on the wealth or paucity of material available
on each author.

633 **Mexico: facts, figures, trends.**
Mexico City: Banco Nacional de Comerico Exterior, 1976.
irregular.
A handbook intended for circulation outside Mexico, attempting to provide
historical, political, economic and social data on the country.

634 **Mexico A-Z: an encyclopedic dictionary of Mexico.**
Compiled by George E. Nelson and Mary B. Nelson. Cuernevaca,
Mexico: Centro Para Retirados, 1975. 832p. maps. bibliog.
A comprehensive dictionary of Mexico's history and culture, from early times to
the present.

635 **Mexico, 1946-73.**
Edited by Dan Hofstadter. New York: Facts on File, 1974.
177p.

A reference book on Mexico, covering history, economy, agriculture, etc. The book is arranged in sections, covering the political administrations from 1946 to 1973, and discussing conditions under each of the leaders.

636 **Northern New Spain: a research guide.**
Thomas Charles Barnes, Thomas H. Naylor and Charles W. Dolger.
Tucson, Arizona: University of Arizona Press, 1981. 147p. maps.
bibliog. (Documentary Relations of the Southwest).

A useful research guide, providing a source book for materials available on Spanish colonial times. The geographical area covered includes all of northern Mexico in colonial times, which means much of the present-day United States, as well as a great part of northern Mexico. Included are guides to documentary collections, as well as much reference data such as nomenclature, weights and measures and lists of colonial offices.

637 **Research in Mexican history: topics, methodology, sources, and a practical guide to field research.**
Edited by Richard E. Greenleaf and Michael C. Meyer. Lincoln,
Nebraska: University of Nebraska Press for the Committee on
Mexican Studies, Conference on Latin American History, 1973.
226p. map. bibliog.

A manual for research on Mexico, including articles by many authors. Unfortunately the book lacks an index.

638 **Research in Mexico City: a guide to selected libraries and research centers.**
Karen Lindvall. San Diego, California: University of California,
Instructional Services Department, 1977. 45p.

An introductory guide to fifteen libraries and research centres useful for the study of Mexican history and literature.

639 **The war with Mexico, 1846-1848: a select bibliography on the causes, conduct, and the political aspect of the war, together with a select list of books and other printed material on the resources, economic conditions, politics, and government of the Republic of Mexico and the characteristics of the Mexican people, with annotations and an index.**
Henry Ernest Haferkorn. New York: B. Franklin, 1970. 93p.
(Burt Franklin Bibliography and Reference Series, 323. American
Classics in History and Social Science, 114).

An early bibliography reprinted from the 1914 edition, of works dealing with the Mexican War, arranged for the convenience of the military student.

640 **Who's notable in Mexico.**
Mexico City: Who's Who in Mexico, 1972- .
A Mexican biographical dictionary in the English language.

Index

The index is a single alphabetical sequence of authors (personal and corporate), titles of publications and subjects. Index entries refer both to the main items and to other works mentioned in the notes to each item. Title entries are in italics. Numeration refers to the items as numbered.

137

140

141

144

147

151

154

156

157

159

161

162

165

Map of Mexico

This map shows the more important towns and other features.

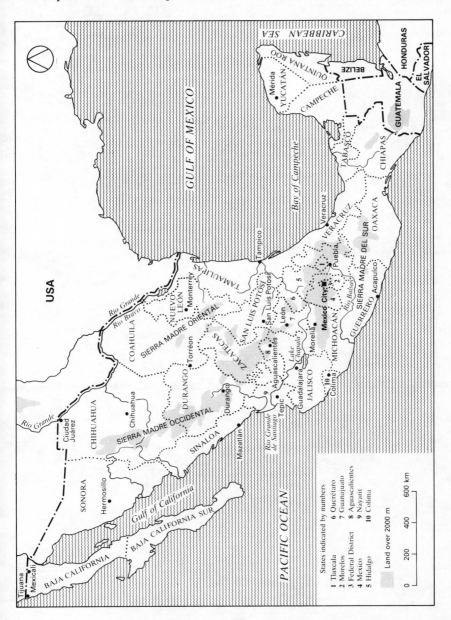

States indicated by numbers

1 Tlaxcala
2 Morelos
3 Federal District
4 Mexico
5 Hidalgo
6 Querétaro
7 Guanajuato
8 Aguascalientes
9 Nayarit
10 Colima

Land over 2000 m

0   200   400   600 km